'Laughter, Madness & Mayhem'

Terry Dicko 'The Mad Axe-Man'

'Laughter, Madness & Mayhem'

Terry Dicko 'The Mad Axe-Man'

www.warcrypress.co.uk
As told to Jamie Boyle (c)

NOTE:

The views and opinions expressed in this book are those of the interviewee, in the main Terry Dixon of Middlesbrough, and obtained during recorded interview and do not necessarily reflect the opinions of the author.

'Laughter, Madness and Mayhem' ISBN: 978-1-912543-16-8

Printed and bound in Great Britain by Clays Ltd, Elcograf S.p.A.

Book Cover Design by Gavin Parker Art – gavinparker.uk

Find out more at: facebook.com/terrydicko/

DEDICATION

I'd like to dedicate this book to my beautiful little Mrs, Leslie Anne Oliver. You're everything to me and the love of my life.

CHAPTERS

"St Hilda's is a mere colony where among the gathered,
are the vilest of the vile".

Local paper, 1859

FOREWORD

Barry Faulkner

Legendary Middlesbrough Club Owner

Where do I start with little Terry?

I first met Terry around the early 1980s and I've drank with and been driven mad by the devil ever since.

One of Terry's favourite things to do is kick his legs up in the air and try to put his leg over people's heads. He's even done it to bloody top DJ stars in my club before now.

I thought as soon as I met Terry that he was already mad! Yes, we've had our fall outs, which maybe at a stretch have lasted a couple of days but we've always been the best of friends when he wasn't plotting to murder me that is.

One time me and him had a fall out and I came back to my house and there was a big fucking 12-inch knife stuck in the front door. The knife was still moving so I knew he wasn't very far away. I knew it was Terry's because it still had margarine on it!

Terry Dixon is absolutely bonkers, and anything can set him off. He's obviously bi-polar and without a shadow of a doubt he has a real touch or pure madness in him but there's genuinely more good than bad in him and I've always cherished the dear friendship we have, he is one of my oldest friends. I say that, but I also have to say there's been times when it's been such a pleasure to go times without seeing him, particularly when it's been a full moon but when I've had breaks from him it's all the nicer to meet up with him and then its nicer still when he goes home (laughs)

Truth be told I've never seen Terry fight, I've seen him threaten loads of people and tell people he'll put an axe in their face though.

If you've ever been in any of my clubs you'll know that I used to have all the best DJ'S in the world coming to play and if Terry was sat in my company I could see the Paul Oakenfold's, Boy George's and Pete Tong's looking over at Terry thinking "Who the fuck is that please keep him away from me!" Terry would drive them mad clicking his hands together or just generally being hyperactive as he usually is.

One thing I can say about Terry is that he's never been a bully. If Terry saw a homeless man he'd take his coat off his own back and wrap it around him because he always backs the underdog in life.

Terry wouldn't see anyone in a bad way. I'd be lying if I said he doesn't have a nasty streak, but it wasn't like Lee Duffy's was. I can speak of him in the opposite tense. Lee Duffy did it for fun where there's more reasoning behind Dicko's violence if he has kicked off anywhere. Terry's like Lee Duffy's love child if you like. Terry's a smaller watered down version of how the Duff was but still very dangerous if crossed like one of them wild coyote dogs.

Terry has been a good friend to me even though I don't see a lot of him now. Since I've retired we've gone our opposite ways as I don't go in my drinking establishments much. I maybe bump into him two to three times a year, but I'll always have plenty of time for Terry.

Terry is different from the other rough faces in the town. Middlesbrough has always had your Terry Dicko's because it's been such a rough place to live in anyone's generation. Terry keeps the run going in the fact that there's still a local madman/lunatic going, and long may it continue. Terry Dicko keeps the Boro fire burning in that sense I suppose.

Terry is unique, a one-off funny character and god can he be funny. Did I mention he can also be annoying? So, he's a bit like Marmite depending on what mood you're in. I'm pretty sure his real names Lucifer though too.

I absolutely have a lot of love for my little mate Terry and I wish him all the success in the world with this book. You deserve it my friend and I hope you have a tremendous future.

Your frenemy Barry x

"Don't get mad, get even."

4

1

Losing Grandad

I grew up over the border in Middlesbrough, the correct term for our once lovely little area was St Hilda's.

I grew up in a warm caring family who showered me with love from a young age. My Mother was Marjorie Bowler-Robinson. My Father was Joe Dixon, he was a Seaman, he was also a real joker of a man and very well respected. I was the spitting double of my Father.

I was born on Inner Street over the border behind St Hilda's School on the 15th of May 1957. I have three fives in my date of birth, but my Mam always said I should have had three sixes in it instead because I was a bit of a devil as a child.

I had two Brothers and two Sisters. My older Brother Brian died 28 years ago of a heart attack when he was still a relatively young many at 36 years old. When I lost Brian, I was absolutely heartbroken; his death completely shattered me as we were so close with there being only three years age difference. I'd lost a brother before, our Joe, but he died before I was born. Even though I never met Joe, I would think of him all the time. I used to talk to our Joe often when I was a child because I believed that if you talk about the ones you've lost it keeps their spirits strong and always around you. My Sisters' names are Rita and Maxine.

Growing up over the border in the 60's we lived in just a small terraced Victorian house, Mam would roll the Gazette up and stuff it in the corners of the windows to keep the draft out and we used to have to get washed in the sink with only an outside toilet in the backyard, but our home was always full of love. Even though we never had a great deal in them days as kids, we didn't know any different.

So, when we moved to a maisonette in the same area it was like moving into a mansion. Having an airing cupboard was like a luxury to us. Our new house had a bath and us kids would all pile in together. Our house was just a built-up shithole really, but we thought it was great.

As a child I was a crazy kid and very hyperactive. I suppose looking back I was a needy child and whatever I wanted as a kid I got. This was down to our Mam and Dad losing our Joe before I was born so they showered me with extra love and I used to get away with a lot that maybe other kids wouldn't. When I was out on the streets putting windows in or mooching in warehouses they wouldn't really give me both barrels like my other friends' parents would give them.

I used to go out over the railway lines on my little journeys and trouble usually followed me.

I think the first time I was ever in the famous Bongo was when I must have been only five years old. It wasn't the

Bongo in them days it was the Kenyon Café but Abduli still owned it. Abduli died only a few years ago aged 104 but he first met me when I was 5 years old.

All the way through my childhood the one thing I was, was pigeon daft. For any child growing up over the border we had the Transporter Bridge on our doorstep, so it was a hive for pigeons.

My daily playground was the River Tees and I'd often be playing on a regular basis with rats the size of Dobermans. Sometimes me and my pals would go out catching rabbits and keep them as pets, I never wanted to hurt any animals I've always loved all of god's creatures. I hated unnecessary suffering to animals, but I was always climbing for pigeons and sometimes right up the Transporter Bridge. I didn't realise at the time, but I was risking my life for skem because one slip down and I'd have been dead instantly, of course everybody in Middlesbrough knows how big the Transporter Bridge is (223 feet) and it's frightening looking back at what I used to get myself up to even when I was as young as maybe seven years old. That was on a weekly basis going in search of pigeons, and me and my little gang of mates would have names for them like "Choca flighty" because it was brown or "Grizzly" because that one had speckles on it and we'd often swap these pigeons that we'd caught earlier in the day like normal kids swapped football stickers. The "grizzlies" were always the hardest to catch but I got the "grizzly" because my determination wouldn't give in and I was always extremely agile climbing up to catch these birds. When I caught these pigeons, I felt like James Cagney (top of the world Ma) I was risking my life ten times over, but I didn't give a fuck because I collected pigeons, if I wasn't out of school collecting them then I'd be in school drawing them and I had to have the best ones over my friends.

Another thing I couldn't be beaten at also when I was a lad was collecting fish. I would go over the gas works near the Transporter Bridge and they'd be huge Koi Carp in there. Well me and my little gang of friends used to go over to the gas works and steal these fish and protecting the place was an old fella we nicknamed "Mad Harry". Why was he called Mad Harry? Well the clues in the name really, he would throw bricks at us and call us all bastards. It's sad to say we tortured Mad Harry and had his life, but we were just kids who loved the chase.

The fish were kept in these two huge tankers maybe 70ft up and we'd climb with our buckets and steal the best-looking fish we could get our little thieving paws on.

In one of the tanks there was one massive fish about fifteen inches long and it was the biggest by far. Me and my mates called this fish "Grandad" and the reason we called it that was that it must have been the Grandad of all the other fish, you just had to look at the fucking size of it and it had these things hanging down from the corners of its mouth which made it look sort of bearded so we figured it was the "Grandad" alright. Well me and my mates had been trying to capture "Grandad" for an absolute age and none of us could get him. That was until I, the little bastard I was, went on my own one day after school, I had to jump in the 4ft deep tank to capture it in my clothes, but I got him, and I was the main man in my little gang of friends that day. My moment of triumph was short lived because one of my friends from school stole "Grandad" from my back garden that very night from the bucket I kept him in. I never did find out who it was that stole my "Grandad". I found that really hard to take because I would often climb up on the gas works on my own just to stare at "Grandad" before I got him. He was like a lottery win, but I had never really thought about what I was going to do with him once I got him, I'd never thought that far ahead.

My Mother wouldn't give a toss for anyone when we were growing up and she protected us all ferociously. My Dad always provided for us and would work long hours on the docks at times.

All us children were brought up to have manners. It was ingrained in me by both my parents to go out of my way to help people. Saying that, I had a real devilment as a kid and I was always doing naughty things and playing jokes on people.

As a kid I was best friends with Nosha Howard and he was the mirror image of me, in fact he was a wind-up merchant too. We'd often be playing pool and when I'd turn around half the balls would be missing, and he'd be going along putting them in with his hands, I knew he was fucking cheating, but he swore blind he never did but I always knew with that fucker.

I love Nosha he's my pal, but he's always had me in trouble right from being kids and then into adulthood. When we were young he'd be saying "ooh he's been speaking about you Terry" many times when people hadn't, just to get me into fights, so he could laugh. So many times, I'd be having fully blown arguments with lads and Nosha would be stood behind my back laughing away and nobody had said a word about me, Nosha had set the full thing up for his entertainment. These days Nosha's a very successful businessman and I still love him, he's a good-hearted lad.

It wasn't only Nosha who made me do some crazy funny things oh no, I've always been quite capable of that myself. I had another friend called Pop Harris who used to wear his hair in a great big teddy boy style quiff. Well me being a little twat, I went home and got some Immac hair removal cream, came back and said, "Are you alright Pop?" while rubbing my hands in his hair. Well of course this stuff makes your hair fall out and I "dequiffatated" him. I just couldn't help myself.

Growing up over the border in St Hilda's it was an extremely rough area in Middlesbrough. Anybody wanting trouble would find it over there. St Hilda's had real hard cases like Peter Woodier and Walter Crockett who were very rough men in a rough dockland area. The place was always full of prostitutes, particularly pubs like The Captain Cook and The Robin Hood was where they hung out. Many prostitutes used to get a great deal of business from the sailors who'd parked up for the night. Looking back, I had a fabulous childhood even though we grew up in a real poverty stricken area. When you think of kids nowadays, they've got phones, laptops, kindle's etc... We never had anything, we always made our own entertainment. I was happy playing among pigeon shit and never cared for anything.

There's a saying that goes, an apple a day keeps the Doctor away. Well when I was growing up I'd have maybe five apples every day because I used to steal them from the docks. The fruit used to come in from the cargo ships and then it would all go to the warehouse on Station Street. Well I had a fabulous knack for breaking into the fruit warehouse and helping myself to all the blood oranges I could eat. Sometimes the manager would just tell me to "Fuck off" but I never got caught much. Some days when I'd break in, I'd eat that much fruit that when I went home I couldn't eat my tea because I was that full and my Mam would go mad with me. Fruit always tasted better when I stole it. Sometimes if I wanted grapes I'd have to break into the other side of the train tracks. Most nights when I broke in I would eat maybe four blood oranges and steal a few for my mates. I'd take my jumper off and use it as a carrier bag. Sometimes I would take oranges just to fling at people for a chase. It was nice to eat so much fresh fruit on a daily basis as I knew my parents couldn't afford to buy us these nice things all the time. It did come natural for me to be a thief I must say, but when you have nothing in life it's called providing for yourself. My Mother and Father really provided for us, but we weren't flush. My dad liked a bet now and then, but he never once put his betting before us. We always came first with him before anything and he was a very good man.

I learnt to swim in the river Tees. My Dad used to take me in there every Sunday and it took me six months to learn to swim. My dad even made a raft for me to float on. If social services were about in them days, then they'd have viewed my old man as a bad man, but it was the 60's and that's what people did over the border. They would never think that it was full of pollution etc... So, when it came to going swimming with the school to the old Middlesbrough baths, I was like a fish. I won everything at school swimming wise, I was an exceptional swimmer like my Dad.

I loved my Dad very much, he let me get away with so much as a boy when I really should have had the belt umpteen times like my mates got. He spoilt me rotten because he knew of the pain of losing a child. He never belted me when I really needed it because he loved me so much.

"Don't let my politeness fool you, this dog bites!"

2

What a Gas!

I went to St Hilda's primary school over the border and my secondary was Hustler School up Acklam way. I was up to all sorts in that school like locking a teacher in the cupboard until she was crying and then I took the class myself! I told her that she'd been a naughty girl but needless to say I didn't last long in that school before I was kicked out.

To be honest I was never very academic and at 13 years old I was moved to Newton Aycliffe Approved School for the bad lads. I left school with no qualifications to my name and I thought it had all been a huge waste of my time attending school in the first place, I was far more interested in chucking rubbers at the other kids' heads.

What I did have going for me in abundance was that I was a little grafter. If I saw any opportunities, I'd be straight in there like a rat up a pipe. I've never shoplifted in my life, I had standards. No, what I'm talking about is warehouses and finding copper them kind of things. I've never burgled a house in my life can I just say. I'd like to think that I've always had strong morals in that respect of committing crime. I always viewed people that were robbing people's houses as below me and rightly so in my opinion. What I would do though was to walk about and see things at the back of warehouses and I'd think, I'm coming back for that tonight. I was very much into things like that. I'd never steal from good honest people never, always the big rich businesses who could afford it.

My first taste of prison was something that really wasn't even something I'd orchestrated. What happened was a lad had nicked a car and I was just the passenger who was getting a lift from A to B when the police started taking chase. Anyway, to cut a long story short the lad smashed into the Newport Bridge and I was given three months.

When I came out I got my first job window cleaning. It was just a way of making a few quid to get me out at the weekend and it was a good laugh. I'd always been fantastic at climbing, so climbing about up people's houses came natural to me.

I was always doing a few naughty things on the side like passing on stolen goods because I've always been one of these people who couldn't stand doing nothing. I suppose that's down to me being so hyperactive.

The other jobs I had in my early years were as a wagon driver, British Steel and on Tees docks. I was on the docks for years with my Dad and my Brother. Working on the docks was a laugh a minute and I enjoyed it because I was always doing things for the craic. One moment I'll never forget was with Billy Duffy (god rest him) and Nosha Howard. Now Nosha has the exact same sense of humour as me, when he'd start chewing his lip that was always a sign he was about to be up to no good.

One day I was working with Billy and Nosha in a Portakabin on the docks and it was break time. Many a time we'd spend it going to sleep on the tables or reading mucky magazines. Well this day Billy was asleep so me and Nosha sneaked out and wedged a piece of thick timber against the door to lock him in. Billy was completely sparko but before me and Nosha left the cabin we turned all the gas bottles on full blast to try and gas him. Anyway, we've sneaked out very quietly and just watched through the cracks of the curtains and after about 6-7 minutes Billy wakes up, cheeks puffed out and ran at the door, of course he couldn't get the door open and he started screaming that he couldn't breathe and shouting "HELP ME". Basically, me and Nosha had tried to gas him for a laugh and we were both sat watching him crying with laughter from outside the cabin. Poor Billy was running about like a hamster trying to suck air in through the doors. After a couple of minutes when we wiped away our tears we let him out. After he caught his breath again, he said, "YOU PAIR OF BASTARDS I THOUGHT I WAS GONNA DIE!" He looked like a chipmunk.

When I was 17 I was sent to Long Newton prison for a month. My Mam and Dad hated me getting sent away because they were both very honest people. My Mam and Dad were very loyal to me and I know I broke their hearts doing the shit I was getting up to in them days. No matter what prison I was ever sent to them two always travelled to come and see me.

When I first started going in pubs when I was around seventeen it was 32p for a pint of Harp lager in them days. Sometimes if I wasn't working I'd go out thieving on a night with maybe three other lads, we'd nick a load of scrap and weigh it in for £40. Anyway, we'd all get done up and go out and get blind drunk with £10 in our pockets.

When I first started going out drinking it was always with the same little gang of John Graham, Nosha Howard and my Cousin Ronnie Bowler and it was nearly always to the Speak Easy (later to become the Havana). Our weekly ritual would be to call in the Boro fish bar on the way there. Most nights when we went out together one of us would always end up fighting, mainly through Nosha starting it just for the wind up.

One night, in The Ship Inn, when I was just a young lad, a drunken sailor came in. Over the border we got a lot of sailors coming in because of how close it was to the port. So anyway, this drunken sailor was at the bar and he was completely arseholed and so decided it was time he left, the fella had had enough. About ten minutes after he'd gone I noticed this envelope at the bar. Me being my usual nosey self I opened it and there was over £400 in it, which as you can imagine was a hell of a lot of money in the seventies. If I'd have known him or even knew where he was I'd have chased after him, but he was long gone. I split the money with the Landlord. Every time I hear the song what do you do with a drunken sailor it always reminds me of that very kind drunken gentleman.

"Friendship and loyalty can't be bought."

3

Holiday in the Big House

The first ever real men's prison I was ever sent to was Durham prison in 1979. Durham gaol was really an old castle and hundreds of years old. It was a truly horrific place and crawling with cockroaches. I was petrified of the cockroaches, many times I would wake up and they'd be in my bed. It was a truly disgusting place. I would be cleaning my cell every day and it never looked any better.

Luckily enough Wakefield's Paul Sykes had just been released from there but there was still a lot of rough men in there. It greatly saddens me how Paul Sykes spent his final days getting pissed on and tortured by kids when he was in the gutter. The little shit-bags wouldn't have had any idea who that man once was and the fear he could instil. There are people who took advantage of him when they wouldn't have looked sideways at him once over.

At the time safebreaker George Reynolds of Darlington, who was hilarious, and James McDonald, better known in Seaham as Jimmy Mac were in there. I clicked with Jimmy and me and him have been friends for many years ever since.

I did 32 months in total of a 4 year sentence because I'd hit a man with an axe. I was charged with Section 18 wounding with intent. The bastards passed me up for parole. Prison's really a terrible place and such an awful environment to be in, I would never recommend it to anyone. If you do prison you never forget it. It takes you years to get prison out of your system. Of course, I've gotten older now and it's very much forgotten about but for years afterwards it was never far away from my thought process, although I can laugh about it now.

I know what you're thinking, I can hear your thoughts saying, "Well what did you do to go to prison you little bastard?!" Well what really happened was it was the 3rd of October 1979 and I'd been out from work on a black un (good drink). I was mortal drunk, and I'd been arguing with my Mrs in my front garden. Anyway, I was having a fully blown argument on the front as man and wife do, when a good Samaritan Jack interfered. Now I wouldn't have minded if I was hitting her, but I wasn't we were just arguing. So, he'd got really involved in something that had nothing whatsoever to do with him! So, I said, "Wait there nosey parker" and off I went to get my axe. Anyway, I came out and went to hit him over the head with it, but he's put his hand up to stop it and it's caught him in the hand. I can't excuse what I did, at the end of the day I was an arsehole drunk and I deserved the prison I got. If I ever saw that lad again I'd buy him a pint. I have no ill feeling whatsoever towards him and I made a mistake. I was in the wrong, I've done my sentence and that's the end of it. I'd like to put that down purely to being young, drunk and extremely foolish.

When I was in prison I got myself a job as a cleaner. Then I went to work in the workshops making football nets and pegs. I was the quickest in the shop, I would make two kilos on the morning alone the screws loved me doing it.

I never once had any trouble in prison. I know people who've written books in the past can tell a load of lies in their books but I'm not one of them. I never had a fight with anyone, I just wanted to get my time done ASAP and get back to Middlesbrough.

I wasn't released back into society until June 1982 and I didn't have a 'scooby doo' what I was going to do. I was back living at my Mam and Dad's and my thought process was just to live each day at a time and try to get a few quid.

Middlesbrough was very much a rough fucking place back in 1982 and the Duffer (Lee Duffy) had just about arrived on the scene. One fella I did meet around that time was club owner Barry Faulkner, John Graham introduced me to him. I've been friends with Barry ever since and I've had some marvellous times with him along the way. One of the things I like so much about Barry is he's got the same mischievous and sadistic sense of humour as me and he's been up to all sorts himself.

Barry once visited a zoo in Florida and accidently knocked a parrot into the crocodile pond and it was eaten alive. It cost Barry over £1000 as before the bird was eaten it grassed him up.

I was also into antiques then, the same as Barry and he was opening bars up left, right and centre we had a lot in common. I would always be selling Barry things, they weren't pinched, they just weren't paid for. Barry to this day doesn't have any idea unless he reads this that is.

At that time in my life I was wild, robbing the warehouses over the years was always very lucrative for me. I worked with one lad and I won't say his name, but they called him 'Nana Carey' he had a big nose and carried a little black book full of gossip. I would say to him "You get in first", he would ask why? Then I'd tell him "It's because you've got more bottle than me". What my thoughts were really is that he'd get caught first if there's anyone already in. Me and him used to rob all sorts and we were very good at it.

Throughout my life violence has never been far away from me, wherever I went. Stabbings, coshings and glassings I was crazy. At times I've done a couple of remands, but I've always managed to stay away from long prison sentences.

One man said to me once "I'm gonna dance on your fucking grave Dicko when you've gone you little cunt". I said "Will ya? Well I'm getting cremated".

I never ever started with any of the violence as well I'd like to say, I've always hated bullies. I've always been a man though who could never sit back and watch people taking liberties with me or my friends. I've had a lot of scraps with people who've tried to take the piss out of me because I'm only 5ft 6, well them people who've put it on me have always got a fucking shock let me tell you.

I was the cleaner in Durham and I was the finest in the whole prison. The cons used to say it was a pleasure to have a shit in the toilets I had cleaned on a daily basis.

I met Fargy Dowell in Durham and he was from Cumbria. Fargy was the last man in this country to get the birch and he used to ask me to get him baggy underpants which I did. Normally in prison when you get asked for something like that by another con you can put another angle on it, meaning to get something in return but that wasn't me and I got them for him.

The daddy of the prison in there at the time was a fella from Newcastle named Fred 'The Head' Mills for obvious reasons, the clue was in the name and he was a big strong man. Most days he would say to me "Can I have your paper after you scouser?" No matter how many times I told him I wasn't a scouse he would call me scouse. It was a bit like how Trigger called Rodney "Dave" for years in 'Only Fools and Horses'.

Freddie Mills would clash with the other prison lunatic Paul Sykes I was told whenever they were in together and one of them was usually kept down the block, so it wouldn't all kick off on the wing. Mario Cunningham from Newcastle and Butch Bulmer from Sunderland were other really hard men in there at the time.

You had to make your own entertainment in jail and one of my favourite past times, when it was time for the roll check at 8pm,was to make sure I would be stood on a chair when the guard looked in waggling my cock and balls back at them at the keyhole.

There really are some vile bastards in prison and one quickly learns to navigate away from the shit and scum. I was talking to one guy in the gym and then somebody quickly ran over to me and said "Don't talk to him that's the Babes in the Wood killer Ronald Jebson" the child killer. On another occasion I started talking to another man when yet again the same thing happened, "don't talk to that cunt its Granny Smith who used to bite off old ladies' nipples". The truth is, in prison, you don't know who's who but very soon I got to know and jugged a few with boiling water mixed with sugar on a morning. As soon as they screamed I ran like fuck to avoid a nicking. This was something a lot of inmates did to child killers, paedophiles and other such pond scum.

"No great mind has ever existed without a touch of madness." - Aristotle

4

Fishing for Business

The 1980s were very good to me, I was always out making money and then partying with it. When I say making money I mean burgling warehouses for antiques or up to something else.

I'll never forget towards the late 80's a friend asked me once, "Terry can you get me some wood?" I said, "Yes of course I fucking can, what size do you want?" He told me "8 x 2s". So, I told him to pick me up at 10am and we'll go get exactly what he needed at my yard.

So, he comes to my house and we drive to the yard. We both get out and load it up and he seems pleased, it's exactly what he'd been looking for and he was over the moon at the knock down price I gave him. So, we're back in the van and I say to the fella that he better put his foot down sharpish, he asked "But why Terry?" I said, "Son it's because that wasn't even my yard and we've just pinched all that wood which is in the back of your van". He screamed and was nearly crying but he did as I asked, he put his foot down right enough and we were off with a load of knockdown price wood and I'd made a few quid. I was always pulling stunts like that almost on a daily basis.

Although during most of my life I've always been involved in crime I've always had a sense of decency about me, now I know that might sound fucking bonkers to some people but it's true.

There's a saying, I think Londoner Dave Courtney says, that there's good baddies and bad goodies. Yes, there's bent police men and yes there's good robbers like me. Say, if I was in a pub and a man had dropped his wallet, I wouldn't fucking dream of keeping it, no I'd end up chasing after him to give it back. I'm not doing things like that to look good in front of anybody else, I'm doing that because it helps me sleep well at night. I've always had goodness in my heart and I'd always go out of my way to help people, so I'd never take advantage of anybody who was down. It was the big rich companies who could afford it as I've said before that would make my eyes shine.

If you're reading this book Jesus then please forgive me Lord, sometimes I do not know what I do. I've always had to go out and earn a few quid it's just how it was, plus I was always out on the pop, so I had to fund that.

What it was with us was that there was a gang of us, like my cousin Ronnie Bowler, John Graham and Nosha Howard and we would always be meeting up for a few drinks. We would usually start off over the border at The Fleece, The Ship Inn, The Captain Cook or The Robin Hood. Then we'd stop and have one in The Grand (Liquor Vaults) I mean town was totally different then to what it is now. Other pubs we'd usually booze in from that point have gone now, like the Shakespeare and The Masham.

In the 1980's Middlesbrough was like the Wild West, it was just full of rough lads who didn't give a fuck! You had people like the Duff, Kevin Hawkes was also a rough lad and his little mate Kev Auer. Both were really lovely lads. John and Brian Graham, Paul Debrick, Kenny Howard, Davey Allo, Boola, Andy Picko, Peter McGee and Joe Livo were all major players in the town who had big names. I was very similar to my friend Lee Duffy in the fact that the older I got the crazier I became.

Lee at 26 was more bonkers than he was at 19 and that's very unusual for a lad because normally lads calm down as they get older. Well I didn't calm down until I was about fifty-five, which was only six years ago! I think in my case and Lee's it was because we were both extremely hyperactive. I think I've calmed down 25 years behind everybody else.

Years ago, I was that busy fucking about and winding people up I never took anything seriously. Nowadays I've noticed I catch myself listening to other people's conversations and being aware of my surroundings, so I must have slowed down and matured and finally grown up.

Saying that, me listening to other people's conversations was how I got so much work when I was working along with Cockerill because sometimes I'd overhear fella's crying in pubs saying they were going get filled in etc and I'd walk over and say "I'm sorry to stop you there son but I couldn't help overhear you saying that you're in trouble! Now me and my mate Brian Cockerill can put a stop to that for X amount of money". I got a huge amount of work put our way from my listening skills alone.

Even though I've calmed down in my life, I still don't stop and I'm always on the go. I no longer jump over the gate I open it and walk through it but my life's still racing at 100mph. That's just what Terry Dicko's about and I'll be like that until my grave.

In Jamie Boyle's book on Lee Duffy, my good friend Barry Faulkner describes Lee Duffy as "a bigger version of Terry Dicko" and I found that hilarious and I could see his point. I had a wonderful friendship with that man Lee Duffy R.I.P.

"Violence is a disease, a disease that corrupts all who use it regardless of the cause".

5

The Scheming Racket

The Steam Packet used to be a public house over the border in a dockland area. Now by the time I got involved with it, it was a derelict building. This lad asked me to do some work in the place and it was when I was waiting to be paid that it transpired that he turned out to be a little shit! He was one lying slink and I was fucking fuming because I'd put a lot of time into fixing this old building up. This fucker had had me doing all kinds to the place and no money was ever going to be forthcoming. In fact, he had no intention of paying me from the very start. When he was telling me his lies he even went to the lengths of taking me to his Solicitors saying I was going to be his partner, so I told him I was up for that. This con merchant thought he was gonna con me like he'd conned everyone else and he must have thought I was just going to forget about it, well this little bastard from over the border was never going to forget about him or leave him alone.

I waited outside on a trip to his solicitors with him, but I could hear 'Billy Bull-shitter' talking to his Solicitor saying, "Can't you just say I own the building?" Then I could hear the solicitor say, "I can't do that!" Anyway, we both left, and I drove him, listening to his lies but not letting on that I knew that he was trying to have me over. Anyway, I waited until we were back in the packet and fortuitously there, by the door, was a selection of walking sticks, I picked one up as he was spouting all his lies to me. I let him babble on for a good five minutes then I said "You lying bastard, I heard every word that was said" then I really give him it with the walking stick, I really went to town on him and told him he was a scheming scumbag and I took the pub off him. Afterwards he even came back and tried to burn it down.

Although I knew that the Steam Packet wasn't his to give away, the real owner Geoff was his friend. I got in touch with Geoff, who was out of the country and had no real interest in the place. I told him that if I had to walk away from this place after making it look like a palace then I was going to make sure it got burnt down. Geoff said to me "Please Terry don't, you have my word you can look after it from this day on". Legally, on paper, I was never the owner but from that day onwards the Steam Packet was mine.

Eventually the police got me out in 2003 and they boarded it up and it was sold to John Graham and Billy Woodier. But what good times from 1995 to 2003 people had in there.

These days it's now demolished but I'd made plenty of money out of 'the scheming racket' as I used to call it. The scheming racket holds some tremendous memories for a lot of people in Teesside today. Lads like Kev Hawkes and Kevin Auer asked me if they could hold their own parties there which I agreed to. One lad asked me if they could have a blues party like Clive Ramsey used to do when the Duff was about, and I said yes also.

When I started with the Packet in 1995 the word quickly went around in Boro and it got busier from day one. What went in my favour I think was that a lot of the black men's blues parties were still on the go like Ramsey's and Salvano's, but they fucked it all up with the prices, so a lot of people thought 'we'll go see Dicko's place'. I fucked their trade up because everybody wanted to come to mine. My place was only open Friday and Saturday and it closed when the last person walked out but there were hundreds in a night. It was fucking heaving each night and people were packed in like sardines.

If you're wondering what the Packet was like, well we had every major criminal in there within a 50-mile radius. I know that sounds scary, but we had good characters, real faces. Docko (Graham Docherty) used to come in and I loved Docko to bits. He'd fight, but he'd be laughing when he fought and that was even with big names. My little mate Chino from Redcar, he's sadly passed now but he used to come in. I used to call him Chino Van Damne. He used to say to me "You don't give a fuck about anything do ya Dicko?" Keith McQuade would come in along with Kev Hawkes, Kevin Auer, Boola, Jamie Broderick, Chrissy Howard, Andy Picko, Neil Booth, Barry Faulkner, Tony Robbo, Bambam Crossling, BJ Crossling, Baldy Kelly and DJ

34

Darren have all come and enjoyed a drink at Club La Steam Packet and we were supposed to have Boy George in once after he had played at The Arena, but he never turned up.

My Dad came in one night as the police were raiding it, so I got hold of my old fella and I walked him home. As I took my Dad home there was a police officer there, now my old fella was a bit of a joker just like I am, and he said to the copper "Excuse me there officer but you haven't seen a little dog around have you we've lost Lassie?" When we walked off the officer quickly got on his radio and I could hear him saying "Dicko and his father have just walked up the road saying they've lost Lassie the dog". Well me and my old fella were bad laughing, we didn't even have a dog. Sometimes I would even leave a workers outfit out the back of the packet i.e. hi-viz vest, hard hat and boots so when the coppers raided it, I'd jump out the back and get changed and kid on I was working out the back as a construction worker on a nearby site.

So many crazy things used to happen in the Packet like when I tried to take a horse in from a nearby field. I couldn't quite get it through the doors, but I did take one in The Ship Inn pub for a bit of company when I was having a drink.

Another time the police took my generator from the Steam Packet just to spite me to cut all our electric off but all I did was to get a cable connected from the site next day and I didn't even have to pay for it so that worked out even better. I think somebody who was working for me must have blew me in because the police found out and wanted to do me for it, but I got told about it before they raided me. I managed to get my own generator in time.

My old fella was very staunch and when he came in the pub he'd insist that he paid for his drinks when I told the barmaids to never accept his money.

Of course, I saw a lot of acts of violence in the Packet. Some for good reason and some that couldn't be helped but I would never tolerate people bullying other people.

One memory that comes to my mind was when Paul Stanton (Stano) put a bogie on a man's hand who was minding his own business and I saw it! Well I was fucking fuming, I told him "GET OUT, GET THE FUCK OUT NOW" and he was like "Nah nah Terry don't be like that". I said, "Come on then clever fucker fight me" and he wouldn't. I said, "You dirty bastard doing that to him", then Stano tried to reason his actions by saying "He was a copper anyway!" I said, "He's not a copper", it turned out he was a farmer minding his own business and Stano thought he was gonna pick on him but not on my watch.

Sometimes the coppers used to come in the Packet plain clothed and I'd spin them lies so they could go back to the office and report what I said. One lad came in once and I clocked him right away, he'd ask me questions then avoided any eye contact, so I quickly sussed him out. I'd tell them all crap like "I've just bought a bungalow up Ormesby Bank 100K cash". I'd never bought any fucking bungalows cash in my life, but I knew it was going straight back to the old bill's intelligence on Terry Dicko, so I often told tall stories to them if I suspected they were in the building.

A lad once stood next to me said to me "Why do you pay for your drinks in here, you own the place?" I quickly kicked him in the ankle and I said, "Do you know him stood next to us?" He replied "No", I said "Well neither do I and they send spies in here".

Going back to any acts of violence that used to break out in the Packet, I would be straight in within a matter of seconds to break it up. I've seen some big rough men going for it in there as well. Lads like John and Neil Howard, Mario and Wisdom have all had their fair share of punch ups in the Packet. Another night Bambam and BJ came in and turned on Baldy Kelly but that was down to them allegedly being on crack cocaine and of course that stuff makes people become overly violent. I've seen mild-mannered men who've never had a fight in their lives, as soon as they start with the sniff they wanna punch everyone so that's why, if people were gonna be on drugs, then I preferred them to be taking ecstasy tablets because them things just made you wanna love everyone.

One memory I have off the top of my head I could tell you was when a group of black men were in and they were working themselves, anyway I'd told them to calm down and one of the guys told me to "FUCK OFF" so I ran in and dragged him and pulled him out the doors but before I knew what was happening, his big 6ft plus mate grabbed hold of me but within seconds somebody had seen what was going on and it was obviously one of my friends because they hit him with a hammer. Then I just went to work on him immediately.

One thing I will admit about the Steam Packet was I had tools hid everywhere in the building, upstairs, downstairs and even under the floorboards because you never knew when it would be kicking off. If you were going to be running an illegal after hours nightclub then the one thing you had to do was to be prepared because you didn't know when it was going to erupt or how violent it would get.

My work description was to stand at the end of the bar drinking a double Bacardi and 90% of the people I had in there were my friends. It's just that you always got the odd arsehole as you do when people have had too much drink, and/or they have been on something.

I never went out of my way to dish out acts of violence and I couldn't afford to because the place was rammed with spies most weekends. Sometimes the spies were put off because they'd heard so many stories of Terry Dicko who runs this place which is a crime haven, when in fact, when they came in, they'd see me glass collecting and cleaning the toilets. I was always on the ball and there was no job in the place I thought was beneath me.

Louis Welsh the gypsy bare-knuckle fighter has also been over for a drink in the Packet. In fact, it was me who introduced him to Brian Cockerill in there and we had a drink together. Brian was a good lad and never caused any trouble in the Packet, in fact it sometimes was the other way around and people would start on him as big as he was.

One-night ex-boxer John Mett and Cockerill got into a fight in my place, Brian was saying to me, "Ere Terry have a word" because John was chewing him as he was getting over excited in drink and of course it all erupted. John Mett to this day says I saved his life by breaking it up.

The Steam Packet would open up usually around midnight and people would start piling through about 12:30am, 1:00am time. Sometimes if there was a crowd in then we'd go on and on until they all left but it would be normally 10am, 11am the next day before we would close.

The Packet, at times was very lucrative for me, but of course it didn't come without police attention and other shit I could have done without. What I will say is that many people who came into my place whilst growing up had the best time of their lives. So many people have approached me and said 'ooh Terry me and my Mrs wanna thank you that was where me and my wife met, and we've been married now so and so many years', well what can I say? I suppose I was providing a service I was like Cilla Black but also, I dare say Terry Dicko is responsible for a lot of divorces, there was so many people who came into my place that didn't end up going home for three days.

I do think, and I've been thinking for a while to have a Steam Packet reunion in my mate David Woodier's place The Lobby, like Andy Picko has done with the meltdown nights. Maybe the authorities would frown upon it having a reunion of people that frequented what was an illegal nightclub on licensed premises, I don't know but I know they'd be a great interest in it.

Overall though my memories of the Packet are good. Yes, they were long hours and the next day, because I drank so much, I did have some horrendous hangovers, but I don't regret running an illegal boozer for over eight years.

For as much money as I ever made from the Packet I spent a fortune and I'll tell you why! I've never been a greedy man in life, even when I had nothing. So, when people came into my place I used to have a tab which I'd put dozens of people's drinks on me. What we used to do was all the staff had a drinks list, but we wouldn't use our real names for when the filth kicked the door in. I used to be Roy, the barmaid would have a different made-up name and so on. Anyway, the next day I'd wake up with my usual hangover to be told "Oh Terry you gave twenty nine drinks away last night under your name". My friend Terry Downes from Grangetown used to say to me when he was in the Packet "Terry you can't make money giving drinks away" but I would always say if I can't give my friends a drink then fuck the lot!

Friendship always meant more to me than money ever did in life. I've had some marvellous friends in life and friends I made from the Steam Packet, are friends I still

40

have today. If people didn't have any money for a taxi home, then I paid Flowers (Steam Packet taxi driver) or Buster to take them home.

I never ever gave a fuck about the police coming into the Packet, in fact it was part of the excitement I think. It was a game of cat and mouse wasn't it! They were the good guys I was the bad guy.

The violence inside the Packet walls, well it wasn't always me. Yes, I had to keep house and make sure it ran smooth but also, I stopped a lot of murders happening as well. One night I caught a lad with a foot-long knife when it fell from his trousers by pure accident. I dread to think of what he had planned to do with that as it looked like one of them evil things the ISIS behead hostages with. I dragged him out and told him never to comeback ever again or I'd stick that knife up his arse.

Another time a lad named Michael Cosgrove was being clever with me for no reason whatsoever. Now he went by the name "Paddy" but sometimes called himself "Paddy Auer". Paddy's father is an Irishman and was very well known in the Middlesbrough area for coaching kids boxing. Now Paddy was in the Packet, but he was dancing all over like a dickhead and he was banging into me dancing. Brian Jaffray told me afterwards that it had been Paddy's plan to put it on me because he'd been in the company of his hero's Kevin Auer and Kev Hawkes, so he was full of himself. Brian had told Kevin Auer that Paddy didn't want to play games with me because I'm a naughty little man. Paddy was obviously trying to provoke me, and he banged into me again and

I've lashed out and hit him but as I've hit him there's been a glass in my hand, so I've glassed him in the face. Anyway, a barmaid had ran and got Paddy who was by now crying on the floor a cloth for the cut. Immediately afterwards from what happened with Paddy Cosgrove/Auer/Hawkins or whatever else he wanted to call himself his mate "Boola" tried to glass me but missed. Yes, I was getting irate with Paddy, and to be honest he was doing my head in, he was shouting that he'd ripped his £70 Chippie jeans when he'd been dancing about like it was my fault, but I just lashed out, I forgot I had a glass in my hand when I've reacted. Afterwards there was supposed to be some big backlash because Paddy was very good friends with Kevin Auer and Kev Hawkes and rumour was that they were looking for me.

The next day I got little Kevin Auer's number from Andy Picko. I rang Kevin up and said what had happened and Kevin Auer was as right as rain with me. He just told me these things happen and that he'd once glassed someone in Blaises and didn't even know he had the glass in his hand like I didn't. The next night Boola came in and he asked my cousin Neil Fairclough "Does Dicko have weapons in here?" He told him "What do you fucking think?!" Eventually that evening I had words with Boola and I told him I admired him sticking up for his friend, but it didn't happen the way he thought and we both had a drink. I've seen Paddy since and although he has little sneaky looks nothing has ever come of it. There were never any comebacks from it towards me that's for sure.

Believe it or not but all kinds used to get found in the Packet and I always handed them back to the rightful owner. I've found wallets and handed them back without even being tempted. One lady, I found her bag with money and when I told her I had it for her she said I can't believe I've got that back and that used to make me a little angry. I'd think why, because I was brought up over the border?!

I've always been brought up very honest, well that's a lie because I'd thieve anything but no, what I mean is I always had morals. Anyone's house or belongings were untouchable to me. I only robbed from warehouses or top companies who could afford it. Yes, I would rob big haulage companies, but I wouldn't shoplift. Shoplifting was below me, I had standards as I've explained before.

One night I found a tweed jacket with 1000 Euros in it and it turned out it belonged to a traveller, but I made sure I got it back to its rightful owner. Some travellers like Wisdom, Henry and Davie Ward, Harker, Neil Howard and Louis Welsh would come to the Packet many weekends.

I had a good time in the Steam Packet on the money it brought. It was me who took the risks and it brought me a certain lifestyle for a certain time. If you ever came to the Packet then you'll remember Flowers, Ray Ducko and Buster ferrying people to and from the place.

One night, Flowers said to me in his West Indies accent "COME ON TERRY MAN, GET ME A FARE BEFORE THE BUSTER MAN COMES". This used to have me in fits of laughter as Buster was like Pac-Man and he wanted every fare in the world.

Poor Flowers is gone now, god bless him, but I have lovely fond memories of him. Many times, I used to ask Flowers to drive people home and I'd pay him when he came back.

Only a few years ago, a girl come up to me and asked me if she could have a word? I said certainly, she said "One night you paid for me a taxi as I had no money and I was stood outside the Steam Packet in the drizzling rain". She asked me if she could buy me a drink and it's nice that people can remember some good things I've done for them.

Yes, I provided a service for the many people of Teesside with the Packet and when it was burnt down many of my friends came to my rescue. Andy Picko sent a wagon with a load of plaster boards to help out. BJ Crossling gave me help as well as the late Kev Auer and my other friend Brian Jaffray. When I started rebuilding the place I sent the word out that I'd be back open in ten days. Well people laughed and said no fucking chance because the place looked like the inside of the devil's lair, but I can tell you now, I was open in ten days and I wouldn't be beat.

My nephew, the little cunt, I told him to wash the doors down with soap because of the smoke. Then rub them down with sandpaper before giving it an undercoat. Well he never because he's a lazy fucker and he just painted over the top of the grease. The first night it was open my mate Paul Lanford came in with a brand new £60 shirt, well he must have brushed past the doors because by the end of the night his beautifully smart shirt was covered in soot. I just laughed and told him to take it up with the management but that he'd get no reimbursements from me.

Every year outside the Packet I would build a bonfire for the kids on the estate. Well one night three arseholes left the Packet and decided to ruin it for them by setting it alight. I saw what they were doing, and I ran over and hit the fire starter over the head with a 4 x 2 till he was out cold. Lee Ward (Mario) filled the other two in. The three were screaming like pigs when we'd finished with them. All my life I've never understood my boxer friends who've trained all their lives to master the art of pugilism. My views on fighting was that I couldn't be arsed dancing about trying to outwit someone when I could just smash someone with an ashtray and get it over with in seconds. I didn't see the point in risking getting my clothes mucky!

"I have never given a fuck for the consequences
of my actions".

6

The Duff

The first time I met the one off that was Lee Duffy, I met my friend, I didn't meet the reputation like others did. The year was 1982 and he was on the door of Rumours, he was a bouncer but was underage, not even old enough to be in the place let alone fight with mature men on a regular basis on the doors. Lee's Mam Brenda worked the cloakroom at Rumours as well as take the money at the front door.

My father had actually been at sea with Lee's old man Lawrie Senior in the Merchant Navy many years before hand.

I suppose I became really close with Lee when he worked on the doors with Dale Henderson-Thyne for Jonka Teasdale and for Barry Faulkner on Blaises door around 1985.

Lee viewed me as a little man who didn't give a fuck and he was a big man who didn't give a fuck! We really did have some great laughs together. Now I never saw Lee every week like Neil Booth, Mark Hartley or Lee Harrison did, but every time we got together we'd have a scream and we'd be winding someone up.

For as big as a rep as Lee Duffy had in his life I was never scared of him. Yes, he was capable of knocking my fucking head off any time he wanted to but he always treat me with love and respect. Many times, I would tell Lee to fuck off, but I never felt like he was going to come and batter me, it was like when you're comfortable with your big brother, that kind of way.

Lee Duffy, if I was to sum him up was 'radged' full of energy and full of fun. He pushed me over one day in the Madison nightclub and I chipped my elbow. I thought you fucking big bastard and I ran at him, but he just started laughing. Then I laughed back.

Lee was my friend and all I can say is good things about him. I once saw Lee stick a £20 note in some old fella's pocket, the old guy didn't know he had it and when he next went in his pocket he pulled out the £20 and he was completely at a loss as to where it had come from saying "Eh, I didn't know I had that, where did that come from?" see, that gave Lee a good feeling in his heart he used to say.

One night over the border I was with Lee and a few mates like John Graham and it was Christmas time but everywhere was shut so we couldn't get in anywhere for ages. Anyway, we tried a side door to the Old Robin Hood pub. Lee walked in shouting "OI! OI! NOW THEN! NOW THEN!" but nobody answered. I think Reggie had it at the time, but nobody came out. We all started making ourselves at home and what I'd noticed is one of the lads started taking the piss downing shots thinking it was gonna be a free bar all night. At that point I shouted, "You can fucking pack that in now, you're all paying for those drinks!" Lee said, "Ya right Terry we've come in here to get out of the cold, we're not gonna fucking rob him as well so get ya hands in ya fucking pockets". Lee said, "Terry you're right" and he made sure everyone paid for their drinks.

One night I was in the old Empire pub (now Swatters Carr) and Lee asked me where I was going as I was putting my jacket on, so I told him I was going home. Lee then said that him and Craig Howard would drop me off, so I got in the car with them. So as the car went past the Newport Bridge I said, "Lee you're going the wrong way to my house!" Lee just turned and smiled and shouted at the top of his voice, "PUT YA SEAT BELT ON YA LITTLE BASTARD, NEWCASTLE HERE WE COME!" He had kidnapped me, and we went to the Kenton bar in Newcastle.

I admired Lee because even though he'd been shot for the second time, and he had a pot on his foot he was out and putting a front on as if nothing had happened. Lee walked up to this big guy and said, "INTRODUCE YOURSELF THEN" and bobbed down to his level like the Hunchback of Notre Dame, the scared fella told Lee his name and Lee stood in front of him and said, "I'm Lee Duffy!" The stuttering lad said he'd heard of Lee and Lee loved that. We had a scream that night drinking while Craig Howard stayed sober as he was driving. Lee had a lot of hangers on and if he wanted anything he'd get one of them to get it for him.

I once, coincidently, found myself in Middlesbrough Police station for a weekend along with Birmingham man Leroy Fischer, who, it is alleged, was the person who shot Lee Duffy the second time he was shot in January 1991. Leroy denied that it was him when I quizzed him and told him that Lee was a very good friend of mine, Leroy said that he wouldn't do something like that as he had once been in Durham prison alongside Lee. I remember thinking at the time that he was full of shit, as they wouldn't have him in there for nothing. Lee later confirmed to me that it was Leroy who had shot him at a Blues party the gun had been pointed at Lee's torso, but he had wrestled with the gunman and the gun had then gone off shooting him in the foot. Apparently, the payment Leroy received for shooting Lee was an ounce of coke!

It has been said that some of the people that crossed Lee have been cursed such as Lee King, Richy Neil, Anthony Allan (Ano) and it seems Leroy Fischer himself has been touched by it as he is now completely blind. Lee did idolise Kevin Duckling whilst he was growing up. Don't Forget Ducko was maybe seven years older than Lee so Lee was very much the impressionable kid around Kevin. Kevin told me that the reason their friendship ended was because Lee wanted to have a fight with him all the time when he'd reached being the No.1 man in the town. Kevin didn't want to fight Lee because I think he'd have known the outcome. Lee grew past him and then turned on him in the end.

The night Lee died all the Geordie lot who Lee had been out with got a good kicking from Lee King and Co., which not many people know about but that's true.

When Lee had his fall out with Dale Henderson-Thyne I was the mediator. One night, Lee came around my house shouting he wanted to fight Dale. To be honest that's how I really got to know Lee through knocking about with Dale, in the end Lee came around my house three times asking me to arrange a fight between him and Dale Henderson-Thyne.

What had happened, Lee told me, was that Dale had been to Lee's girlfriend's house when he was in prison to ask for £130 that Lee had owed him. Now this offended Lee greatly and he was furious when he found out, "Please Terry can you sort a meeting, please Terry I can only ask you" he begged. I didn't want to get involved because they were both my friends. In the end I said I'd go and see Dale and with that Lee hugged the life out of me and was shouting "THANK YOU THANK YOU TERRY I FUCKING LOVE YOU TERRY".

Anyway, I went around to Dale's house and found him there, he'd been digging an extension with big Woody at his house all day. Now I didn't know how to approach the subject, how did I break it to him that basically I'd come around to give him the bad news that Lee wanted to fight him. I think, if I remember rightly, even Dale said, "You're very quiet Terry", but I didn't want to say anything in front of big Woody, so I asked if we could have a word in private. When me and Dale got some privacy, I was thinking there's no easy way of telling him, so I just came out with it "Looka Dale, Lee Duffy's been around my house three times, telling me he wants to fight you!" Dale's response was "Go get him then!" I said, "Look Dale you've been digging holes all day leave it till tomorrow". Dale was determined though and told me to go get him right away. I tried to sort it out with the pair of them as I didn't want to see them fighting. I told Dale "We're all friends together" but his reply was still "Go get him". So, I did as I was asked, and went and found Lee at his girlfriends' house. I knocked on the door and I could hear Lee coming shouting "OI OI". Lee stood back, arms folded and asked what had went on! I just told him "He's told me to come and get you" and with that Lee starts shouting "AAAAH MATE THANK YOU" whilst picking me up and throwing me in the air. Lee was ecstatic and said a dozen thank yous.

At the time Lee had this Mark 1 Granada so he set off to follow me to Dale's house. Anyway, we arrive at Dale's and Dale comes out and him and Lee went off ahead of me and around the corner. Afterwards I asked Dale what had happened when they were both out of sight. Dales words were "I wouldn't like to go for another walk with him, he was just too strong". Lee said something different to what Dale said but I never commented on it. Both were my good friends and I was loyal to both of them.

It's been over 27 years since Lee Duffy died and people are still talking about him, because he was the monster of Teesside, but he was a good-hearted monster.

When Lee walked in the pub the rats would walk out. What hurt and annoyed me is the amount of crap people said about him only after he died.

Lee knocked Micky Salter (God rest him) out outside The Havana. Lee didn't half crack him and I went to pick Micky up, Lee was shouting "Leave him Terry" but I couldn't. I picked Micky up and rested him against a shop window for him to regain his senses. Afterwards Lee said I was too soft hearted and was laughing at me. That was all over Micky having a go at Lee's close friend John Fail. As soon as he saw Micky Salter he shouted to John "LOOK WHO I'VE FOUND" then 'BANG' and it was lights out. God bless him but 10 years after Lee's death Micky Salter was murdered at a BBQ in Saltersgill. A few years after Micky's death Paul Salter, Micky's brother came up and thanked me in The Zetland. He stripped a beer mat off and wrote on it the words "Terry, thank you very much". I found it amazing that he did that and I told him I lost my brother too, so I knew what he was going through. I still have that beer mat today.

Lee also knocked Podgie Foreman out in The Ship Inn. As soon as Lee saw him he said "Ooh look who's here" then hit poor Podgie that hard he came back on himself, going full circle and then hit the deck out cold.

I saw Lee hit some poor fella outside the Bongo because he was having trouble with the owners of the club and they barred Lee out. As soon as the club closed for the night I went over Petch's yard to get two full drums of red diesel, I also got a load of concrete to cover the doors of the pub and pulled the signs down and let rocket flairs off because Lee was my pal and I was supporting him, loyalty means everything to me.

Derek Beatty was driving over the Ormesby Bank in Middlesbrough that night, about four or five miles away from where I let the rockets off. Derek saw them and said to the passenger in his car "Dicko must be kicking off again over the border" and he was right. I was barred out of the Bongo for 14 years over it!

There are people that might disagree, but Lee's father Lawrie was a hard case you know! I introduced Lee to my old man and told him that he was Lawrie's boy because my old man had been such good friends with Lawrie from their travels around the world.

Lee's death hit me very hard. When he was laid in his coffin at 6, Durham Road in Eston I said to his Mother Brenda, "I'm not being rude or disrespectful, but Lee wouldn't want Davey Allo doing life for this, I hope to God I haven't disrespected you". Brenda told me she was glad I had said that, and she told me how much their Lee loved me, and Lee had told her I was the most genuine man he'd ever met. Brenda even told me she was going to write a letter to the judge to say that Lee wouldn't want anyone doing life for his murder. For me to go in someone's house and say what I did to Brenda whose son was in a coffin, that was straight from the heart and she could have taken it very differently, thankfully she didn't, but I also told her I loved Lee and he was my good friend.

Lee's funeral was a marvellous send off it really was. Two coaches from Newcastle came, along with some of Leeds top faces Joel Richardson and Marco. It was a very sad day and afterwards the do was at The Oak Leaf on Normanby Road. I had a really good drink and it dawned on me that of all the people that were there, Lee wasn't. I was utterly broken that day.

The thing that stuck in my mind after Lee's death was that Lee's younger brother used to wear Lee's flying jacket. When I saw that my heart used to go out to Lawrie because I realised he was just trying to be near his brother. I mean I lost my brother the year before in 1990 so I knew what he was going through. I suppose wearing Lee's jacket was like him giving him a hug. I acknowledged that straight away, that he wanted to feel close to his brother.

I once chatted up one of Lee's sisters on the wind up and told Lee "It's only because I wanna be your brother-in-law". Lee shouted "YOU LITTLE BASTARD" at me but he was only ever playing with me.

Although he was a big powerful lad I was never scared of him because we loved each other. Sometimes Lee would come and see me at The Ship Inn and Pat the owner used to say to Lee "Any trouble out of you and I'll slap your lugs". Lee would fluster because it was a woman and say, "Honest Pat you won't hear a mouse's fart out of me". I'd give it ten minutes and I'd shout, "HELP HELP PAT HE'S STARTING HE'S JUST PUNCHED ME" and Lee would be shouting "I'M NOT

PAT I'M NOT" like a little scared boy who thought he was in bother.

Many a time I saw Lee walk in The Havana and the crowd would open up like a wild animal was on the loose. You'd have thought a 7ft wild bear was walking about judging by people's reactions to Lee when there was never any need to be like that. People used to look at Lee on the sneak and they were astounded by just looking at him. Lee was like a tide coming into Middlesbrough and he was always at the top of his game for them years and died at the top of his game.

Lee died at 26 and never got the chance to decline like Paul Sykes who used to get beat up by kids because he once had an awesome reputation. The last few years of Sykes' life he wondered about, pants full of piss and didn't know what day it was, that was never Lee thankfully.

I've been good friends with Davey Allo also over the years. I caught up with him only a few years ago in The Zetland pub doorway. I said to him "Do you know what your problem is Davey? It's that you're too predictable". Davey then said "Do you know what your problem is Terry? You're a psychopath!" (laughs) I really like Davey Allo and it's been very unfortunate he's had some awful luck at times himself.

Davey told me he didn't want to kill Lee, he just wanted him to go away, which of course Lee was never going to do unless he was unconscious. There's only a few that know this, but Davey still lights a candle in church for Lee to this day.

In the last couple of years, I've only found out I'm some sort of relation to Davey and when we see each other now we say, "Now then cuz". Davey's a great lad and I know my friend Lee would have forgiven him for what happened, it was just an accident.

It was nothing to do with Davey, he wasn't celebrating by any means, but when news of Lee's death got out around Middlesbrough the town was alive with joy. All the shithouses were having "The Duff is dead" parties. I know of a few people who had done that, and I thought 'you scumbags. They were all little rats who came out of their little hiding holes now Lee had gone.

I was in the pub once with old Davey Allo (Davey's dad) and I liked old Davey. Anyway, I pulled him to one side and I said, "Can I have a word with you Davey please as on three separate occasions you've blanked me, have I done something to you? Please tell me so I can apologise!" He said, "Yes you were Duffy's mate". I said, "Yes that's right and I'm proud to have been". I was never like the rats who distanced themselves after he died and started kissing other people's arses! I said, "Let me tell you something Davey" and then I relayed the story that Brenda was going to write a letter to the judge saying she didn't want young Davey doing life. "ARE YOU HAVING ME ON" old Davey said? I said, "Davey I don't tell lies I'm a genuine man" and he couldn't believe it! Old Davey is sadly no longer here now but he was a good man and he's still missed today.

On the trial itself, I never went. It would have been too painful, and I didn't want to listen to that. I didn't want to hear how my friend died and I didn't want young Davey Allo doing life, so I stayed away. There were no winners in that trial they were both losers. Davey's got to live with it and Lee's lost his life. I get on well with young Davey Allo and that lad has had to deal with tragedy himself. Davey is a straight-talking fella and if something's on his mind he says it as it is. He doesn't suffer fools gladly and I'll always have a lot of time for Davey. God bless Richy Neil, Lee King and Ano who all lost their lives but had something to do with the trial. People say it's the curse of Lee Duffy from the grave, I don't know.

He was my friend and I loved him, I even said to him one day "You know you need to be careful because you're gonna end up dead". Lee just stood up in a big pose like He-Man like he'd just won the Olympic Gold and shouted as loud as he could "I LIVE BY THE SWORD AND I'LL DIE BY THE SWORD" whilst having a right laugh.

I still have arguments today with people because he was my friend. I'm not just not going to sit and have people call him because he's not here.

People only know about Lee Duffy what they want to know, they don't know the loyal friendly Lee Duffy. Lee could be soft hearted, he had a really good heart. For years I put flowers on Lee's grave. Buster Atkinson goes to this day.

There's one story I'll tell you about old Buster whilst we're on the subject. Well Lee Duffy and Lee Harrison once spiked Buster with acid. Buster's always had a taxi firm but at that time I think he only had around five taxis. Well the two Lee's got Buster that off his box he was shouting in the pub "COME IN CAR 43". Lee Duffy and Lee Harrison were crying with laughter. Poor Buster ended up in hospital and Lee was shitting himself at the thought that he might have done Buster in.

Lee Duffy was always spiking people. At John Graham's wedding at The Marton & Country Club he spiked Brian Andrews with a couple of acid. I was there. Lee had a tracksuit on at one of his good mates' weddings. That was Lee.

Lee used to love a dance in The Havana nightclub and to be honest he wasn't the greatest dancer. His best friend Lee Harrison was, god he was smooth and had great rhythm but when I would watch the Duff on the dance floor, usually on his own as it would clear sharpish when he got up, he reminded me of a new-born giraffe trying to walk for the first time.

Lee never spoke to me about being bullied as a child. Looking back with hindsight I don't think he could tell me because he had such a macho image, but I could sense there was something in his eyes regarding his past. Saying that Lee was capable of showing his emotions because he came up to me in the Mayfair club in Newcastle in tears one time. The week before this we had been out, and I lost a chain which was of great sentimental value to me, Lee had found it, picked it up and flogged it but at the time he didn't know it was mine. A week later he came up to me totally distraught and crying saying, "Please forgive me Terry but I found your chain and I sold it". Lee didn't even have to say anything because I'd never have known that he was the one that found it, but he was in bits because of what he'd done. I told him he didn't need to express his emotions to show how genuine he was, and I gave him a cuddle and told him I forgave him. I owed him £250 but he said, "Keep it Terry it will make me feel better".

Lee Duffy was a cunt for winding people up. He pulled my best mate Nosha in the passage way of The Ship Inn and said, "I've heard you've been sayings things about me Nosha is that right?" Immediately I've jumped up and shouted "WOAH, WOAH LEE LEAVE IT, don't you fucking dare Lee he's my best mate leave him alone". Lee turned to me and smiled and said "Terry I'd never fall out with you. Anyway, I'm only winding him up". By this time poor Nosha's heart rate had gone sky high and he didn't know if he was coming or going because he thought he was about to be done in by Lee Duffy. Lee hadn't even any plans on doing any such thing it was just a big joke to him.

Another favourite game Lee used to like playing was smashing half pint glasses over my head when I wasn't looking. One night in The Ship Inn over the border Lee smashed 3 glasses over my head from behind, each time he said "AND AGAIN" whilst laughing his head off like a school kid, my response was "Aah you big bastard" while rubbing my head and laughing along with him. I know that might sound crazy to some people, but we were just young lads and we used to do crazy things to each other.

One night in the pub after Lee had been shot, he was half asleep with his head resting on the table and I made a big bang by throwing a lighter in the fire and Lee shit himself thinking he was under fire again, it was just after he'd been shot the second time and he was on his crutches, I couldn't stop laughing and he was calling me all the little bastards under the sun while hobbling around the pub on one foot chasing me.

One night in The Havana I saw Lee taxing a young kid named Adam. He's no longer here he got killed on a motor bike bless him. Anyway, I went and asked Lee to give him his stuff back because the lad's Dad was a good friend of mine. Lee stood up and said, "Terry he should know better than to come on my turf and start dealing drugs". He then turned to Adam and said, "You're lucky I haven't knocked you out kid, here there's £20 come in here again with drugs and I will fucking hurt ya". I then said to Adam, "Listen he's right". Then Lee shouted to Adam "The only reason you got £20 back of the £80 I've stole is because I love Terry Dicko".

Whenever I saw Lee out in clubs he would run over like a big Doberman and shout "NOW THEN NOW THEN" whilst rubbing my hair. He thought a lot of me, as I did him.

Funny enough I was talking to a lady only the other week and she was telling me how she once went on a date with Lee. She said Lee was a charming gentleman and told her to sit down and that nobody would bother her that night. She told me for the full date people in the pub were getting up shaking Lee's hand it was crazy. She'd never seen anything like it you'd have thought he was royalty.

If you want me to describe Lee Duffy to you, he was just one big tornado in Teesside. He was capable of battering people and full of fun with it.

I miss my friend greatly to this day and I pull people up sometimes when I hear them slating him. It was only the other month that I heard some little scrote slagging him and I said, "Hang on a minute son can I just stop you there, did you know Lee Duffy?" To cut a long story short this lad was 3 years old when Lee died, and he was just jumping on the bandwagon like the rest of the fools in Teesside.

In the early 90s when Lee's grave was getting smashed up I saw one of the main culprits in the Madison Night Club. The Eston man came up to me saying "Alright Dicko?" I said, "Don't you alright Dicko me you cunt! You and your mate smashed my mate's grave up". He was giving me a load of excuses as to why he did it, but I told him to fuck off away from me. I'm as upset about that still today as I was about it when it was happening on a regular basis.

Lee did make me laugh though when I walked in a pub with him, he'd stage whisper to me "Ere Terry watch this" and as soon as people saw Lee they'd get up and run to the doors like rats up a drainpipe. In the end it would get to the point where it was me and him sitting together drinking. I said, "Ere Lee where has everyone gone you've emptied the pub, the full Empire pub". Lee really used to see the funny side of everyone scattering away from him and it made him laugh. Lee used to do a running commentary like when you're listening to the horse racing "and he's almost there now at the final fence, but here's another coming along at the far end and he's at the finishing line of the front door and he's out of the pub and home to win the cup" etc... He was a funny, funny man without him even trying to be funny.

Lee Paul Duffy is fucking irreplaceable and the loyalty I've shown my friend since he's passed is a testament to the love I had for the lad. They say if you speak about the departed, it keeps their spirit and energy strong. My fucking friend will be here forever, and my friend Lee would be absolutely loving the book 'The Whole of The Moon' that has been written about him. A book on the Duffer was a long, long time overdue. The book tells the true story of who Lee really was and what he was about.

Friendship and loyalty mean everything to me. Sometimes in life you've got to dig through a mountain full of shit to find good folk. When you find them you stick by them, well Lee Duffy was good folk. He was the monster of Teesside, but he was our monster.

In fact, when the book 'The Whole of The Moon' came out a friend of mine came over to me and I was with Jamie Boyle. He said he'd bought the Duffy book and read it in 24 hours and that he now looked at Lee Duffy in a different light. I thanked him, and that to me is exactly what it's about, people knowing the real Lee Duffy warts and all. Yes, Lee was a fucker and he'd get up to mischief and he liked to knock people out, but he was still my friend. I spoke with Lee's youngest daughter and his only son and his daughter expressed her views that she was a bit worried that a new book was coming out and that it would bring all the past up. I told her that the book Jamie Boyle's done on her dad is not about that, it's about letting people know the real Lee Duffy. Yes, Lee done wrong but as I always say, "Let him without sin cast the first stone".

I'm very pleased and delighted that now there's a book that tells people about the real Lee Duffy not to mention that the book supports Scope a charity chosen by Mark Hartley who I also love a great deal. I recently spoke with a barrister who knew that a book was coming out on Lee and she said she'd seen pictures of Lee laying dead in the morgue. Some fucker had decided to show her them which I found disgusting.

One of the most disgusting things I've heard, and I only heard this recently, but it was from a reliable source is that Tommy Harrison shit on Lee from the grave. I've expressed my views on Tommy in this book, but I'd like to say this again, Tommy Harrison is one treacherous bastard in my opinion! Now considering he paid for Lee's funeral he's shown that he sheds more skins than a snake and he was supposed to be Lee's close friend.

Now before I reveal what I'm annoyed about I'd like to tell everybody about the time Lee climbed over the wall out the back of Tommy's place at Orchard Way in Ormesby and he looked through the window Tommy was in the front room with a Cleveland Police detective. Lee never ever trusted Tommy after that. I know Brenda blamed Tommy for getting Lee involved with the drugs scene.

When my son Terry was in jail and he had a mental breakdown, Tommy Harrison turned his back on him. Buster who was inside with them at the time said, "We can't just leave him its Terry's son", Tommy's reply was "You can't help him, leave him". That was what our close friend Tommy Harrison said on the situation. Now, what I've only just found out was, in the trial for Lee's murder in February 1993 Davey Allo was fighting for his life and for Tommy to do what I've been told he did well I find it fucking disgusting! What is supposed to have happened is that the prosecution was looking for a picture of Lee looking ferocious standing like a fighter. Well what I'm told Tommy did was to hand one over to the prosecution team, a picture of Lee that nobody had seen before, it was one that allegedly stood on Tommy's fireplace and is of Lee in blue shorts standing in a boxer's pose. What I was told was that when Tommy gave it to the prosecution he said to them to make sure nobody finds out about it! I've only just found out but the source it's come from is very reliable. I just think what a dirty fucking low life Tommy Harrison is if he did pull a trick like that. It turned my stomach when I was told that I can tell you.

Since Lee died there's been all kinds coming forward saying all kinds of things about Lee but the most peculiar was a lad named "Planty" from Redcar. One day I walked in the pub Last Orders and the barmaid Fiona told me that I'd only just missed Lee Duffy's son by seconds. Now I knew Lee had a son, so I asked where he'd gone, and she said just around the corner at The Zetland. So, I walk in expecting to see Michael when in fact I see a lad in a hat. Fiona had told me that Lee's son had been wearing a hat, so I shouted to the lad when I seen him "Are you Lee Duffy's son?" and he shouted back "YES I AM WHY" in an aggressive manner. Now I loved Lee but something about this lad's attitude I didn't like. So, I said "Get your fucking cap off and let's have a look at you!" I said "While you're at it take your glasses off as well. I'm Terry Dicko and Lee was my good friend" and straight away he's said, "Alright you've found me out, I'm not really". I told him to "Leave my friend rest you fucking imposter". Lee would have laughed about it I'm sure.

Stephen Richards wrote the books on Lee Duffy purely for greed and gave that much misinformation out because he didn't know our friend. It was only a compilation of old Gazettes articles. He really is a poor excuse of a man and now he's found god and even went on record to say he shouldn't have written the books in the first place. He really should apologise to Lee's family.

At last the truth has come out in Jamie Boyle's book The Whole of The Moon. Many people have come up to me on the back of that and said it changed their opinion on Lee Duffy.

"You're only given a little spark of madness. You mustn't lose it." - Robin Williams

7

Big Bri, Big Bri, Big Bri

I met Brian Cockerill through Lee Duffy. How it came about was that I was working in The Havana during the day fixing it up and doing a bit of maintenance for the owner Brian Andrews. So, one day I was sawing a big lump of wood, which I was going to use to board up something, and Lee Duffy came in to see me. This was around the time he was running about with Brian Cockerill taxing everyone and Lee had introduced me to Brian by saying "This is my little mate Terry 'The Mad Axe-man". I nodded to Brian who was stood there in his black leather jacket, he wasn't the big hulk that he became at that time though, in them days he was still a little lad before he was on the growth hormones. Don't get me wrong Brian back then was fit looking and quite muscular, but nothing compared to what he was to become.

Now I've read Brian's books and what really happened in the fights between himself and Lee isn't how Brian portrays it in his book. Over the years when I was Brian's partner I told him on many occasions to let Lee Duffy rest. If you ask me Brian couldn't lace Lee Duffy's boots and I'm embarrassed that I worked with him for so many years. Brian's very narcissistic and loves to talk about himself, sometimes in a third person "Ooh Big Bri this Big Bri that". Many times, he would talk to me and I would hold the phone up to the sky whilst he was talking because it was always "BIG BRI BIG BRI BIG BRI" etc...

Brian and I haven't spoken for 3 years because he shit on me, because when I was on a break with my little Mrs he told her to get rid of me, but once over we were friends.

Brian Cockerill was once a good-hearted lad and he was never greedy, and I've had some fabulous nights out with Brian.

Me and Brian used to get up to all kinds when we were on a night out and I was always playing jokes on him.

Many times, when me and him were debt collecting together he'd have to say to me "Listen Terry don't be pissing about on this job" because I'd be forever sneaking up behind him and pulling his trousers down or breaking out in a different language and I'd start doing karate moves in the middle of the room just to embarrass him.

One of my favourite things that I liked doing was lifting my foot over people's heads who were 6ft plus, I used to do it to Brian. I once did it to Paul Sykes about 1991 in The Havana.

Me and Brian worked together for over 20 odd years. How our working relationship worked was that I used to be the talker and he stood there growling looking like Brian does all 6ft 3 of him and 22 stone. A lot of the time when I was working with Brian I was forever finding us work by listening in to other people's conversations in the pubs, sometimes maybe they'd be having a little problem and I would suggest me and Cockerill could make that go away for a little sum of money. Cockerill never brought the work in it was nearly always me.

With Cockerill I never ever gave up when I got a job. Even when Brian used to say come on Terry wrap it in now the blokes long gone I wouldn't. Brian used to say to Leslie my Mrs I wish I could be more like Terry because he never gives up on anything.

One job in particular I did was when I chased a man for three years and everybody thought he was well gone. A friend of mine Jack Wardle told me a story which was that he'd had this poster from the early 70s from the Northern soul artists from America which was all signed. Jack told me he gave it to a lad to show and the lad had it away. Well anyway about three years later I was walking past Annie's bar, the old gay bar next to McDonalds in the town when who did I see but the fella on the run. Well I marched over to him and said just the man I want to see! Where's Jacks picture? He was full of excuses but what I did was march him to his flat which was just around the corner in a nearby flat on Grange Road. Not only was the poster there but he had a book which was all signed by the artists because Barry Faulkner told me he had that as well, so I got both from him and called him a slippery little cunt. I chased

71

that man for three years and once I get something in my head I just don't let it go. So, I got the picture by myself, I didn't need Brian who was asked as well to retrieve it. So, the next day I walked in The Pig Iron pub with the retrieved items in hand. I walked over to Jack Wardle and said, "Look at these two Jack I've just got them out of the charity shop". Straight away he looked and shouted, "THEY'RE MINE THEM THEY'RE MINE". I said they're not yours I've just bought them out of the charity shop. He still insisted that they were both his, but I said there weren't. Even when Jack and Brian told me to give up I wouldn't, and I told Jack that I'd been on this job for three years so it's mine. Brian then came in the pub and told Jack it was mine because he remembers Jack telling me not to bother. In the end I put it on the internet and was offered daft money, but I found out it was fake so didn't sell it. Jack had signed all the signatures himself and never told me. I told him "You dirty cunt, you dirty fat bastard Jack" but I couldn't help but laugh at him. Jack's sons a copper as well I should report him for that (laughs). In the end I think we gave it back to the lad we took it off and didn't tell him it was fake.

When me and Cockerill fell out he was telling everyone I had him over with the picture the narcissistic prick. I don't know how he dare the amount of times I caught Brian doubling back on jobs with me the scheming scumbag.

When Brian released his book 'The Taxman' in 2007 with that story teller Stephen Richards, it was described as 'The true story of the hardest man in Britain'. What I'd like to know is how did Brian work out where he was in the rankings of 'Britain's hardest'?

In his book he mentions me and Lee Duffy, and I'll quote the book:

"On the Saturday night, we went to the Belmont, Freddy Vasey's pub. I said I was Brian Cockerill and we were introduced to all the Middlesbrough people that we were sitting with. People were beginning to realise who I was; they knew that I'd had a fight with Lee.

At the Havana club in Middlesbrough, Lee reached out his hand and offered me a fucking little half a tablet. 'What is it?' I asked. Just have half, you'll be all right,' he told me. I was 26 and I'd never had a drug in my life. He gave me this biscuit; it was called ecstasy, I didn't know what it was and the next moment I was all fucking cabbaged! I didn't know where I was at and I thought, 'Fucking hell I've got to sit down'. So, I went to the car and Lee was like a fucking lunatic, jumping about while I was sitting there fucking monged. I was watching him, and he was looking at me dead concerned and looking after me. I was absolutely cabbaged, Lee shook my hand and said he would never fight me again, like you do when you're kids. If he'd wanted to he could have taken a liberty, like he had with other people in the past, and brayed me all over. No, he perhaps thought, but I don't even think it crossed his mind.

He said, "This lad, here, this lad would stand with you and die with you" that is what he used to say to Mark Hartley and people like that, "see the big fella, he would stand with you and die with you".

We met a lad called Terry Dicko. He was only little, and he was mad, doing all these kicks and dancing and jumping about and having a bit of a laugh. Lee said to him 'Here, he is the best fighter I have ever met in my life. He beat me that day, you know. 'There's nobody can beat him' Lee was saying that to Terry and people in the pub, and, 'He is the best, he is the real deal in boxing terms'.

I'll give Lee Duffy his due; later on, when we got to be friends, he said, "That day you beat me was the first time in my life I had been beaten and I couldn't sleep for weeks on end thinking there's someone better than me in Teesside".

*** Excerpt from 'The Taxman – The True Story of the Hardest Man in Britain by Brian Cockerill. ***

Well let me just say what a pack of shit that is Lee Duffy never told me anything of the sort, Lee never buttered up to anyone like that, all that shit only ever happened in Brian's imagination!

Brian is a sneaky two-faced cunt, at times he would tell the people paying us that I took all the money which was always absolute shit. Me and him were in it together and it should have been 50/50. I speak the truth and he knows where I live if he's not happy.

Me and Cockerill looked after many Tom, Dick and Harry for many years in Middlesbrough and people felt safe coming to us and bringing us their problems because they knew we'd sort it officially.

It wasn't always kicking down doors me and Brian used to do. We took on all kinds of jobs like chasing people over stolen dogs etc... As I've said we got all kinds of work and much of our relationship was down to me being the bread winner.

I did love playing jokes on Brian and one memory springs to mind is when we went to see a sheep breeder for a job and this sheep we were looking at had a problem with its balls, they were huge, and it couldn't walk properly. I shouted, "LOOK AT THAT SHEEP BRIAN IT WALKS LIKE YOU". We both had a good laugh, Brian could always take a joke.

Sometimes I even went along on Brian's guest appearance jobs with him.

Another job me and Brian were called in for was a D.J. who had been had over for all his gear which he'd left in the pub that had hired him. We did collect his debt, but the job wasn't worth what he was paying us, so he called it evens but he was happy that the culprit hadn't got away with robbing him.

Me and Brian were hired by an Asian fella saying he'd been ripped off by some bloke. So, when we got them together it turned out that the Asian guy who'd employed us actually owed the money to the victim in all this so Brian made the Asian guy go find us the money for lying in the first place and he paid us £1000.

Me and Brian would always laugh because the people who were hiring us would always say it wasn't about the money it was the principal of the matter and they didn't like being had over. Brian used to say, "That's fine, you keep the principal and we'll keep the money".

Another time I rang him and told him I had a job for him. Brian told me to see if I could get him a grand to pay his mortgage and I told him I had it. He said he'd give me £200 for getting him it but I said "Guess what Brian?" Would two grand be better than one? He said, "Ooh you haven't?" And I said, "And guess what my friend would three be better than two?" Again, Brian was almost in tears saying "Aah my little mate you haven't" "And guess what my friend" I said, by now Brian's eyes have lit up like a kid in a sweet shop and he said, "What have you got me four?" I said "I'm sure I haven't you fat faced snorting cunt. I've put a grand in from me and I want the two hundred quid" and he laughed, but what Brian did from that deal was to get a lot of money in but then he bumped me for my money. Now you don't do that to friends, but I forgave him because I believe he was on crack at the time.

Brian's even turned traitor on me over jobs with the biggest liar in Middlesbrough Tommy Harrison. Even when I was heartbroken over my Mrs and people said to Brian "Go see your mate Terry he's heartbroken over his Mrs" I was told his response was "Fuck going to see him he's unhinged".

It's funny because when me and him were working I was even threatened with myself by an Asian taxi driver who shouted that he'd get Terry Dicko and Brian Cockerill on me!

Many of the debts me and Cockerill got we'd start off by knocking on the door and when they'd open the door we were very civil but at the same time we had to let them know, and I quote myself many times in them situations as saying, "We are the naughty people". One day we went to pick up, shall we say, a 'naughty tool' and when the man wouldn't get it pronto Brian slapped him with an open hand and knocked him right across the room. Now we shot ourselves in the foot after that because when he woke up we couldn't get any sense out of him to tell us where it was because he was just mumbling and stuttering.

How I ended up on his television program, Macintyre's Underworld, well that was done a bit sneaky by him in my opinion. I was on the phone to him the day before and he never even mentioned that he would be coming down to The Ship Inn over the border with Donal MacIntyre and his film crew. It was underhanded the way he went about it. So, the next day I was in the pub with one of my mates when he turned and said to me "Terry your pal Cockerill's outside with a film crew" I was in Marie McPartland's funeral wake. Of course you seen what was said and that was when I got the rights for the phrase "catalogue look" but that was sprung on me and I didn't have any idea I was about to be interviewed for national television because Brian's narcissistic and all about him so why would he, but I don't think he was happy in the end because I'd stolen some of his sunshine. As I've said my part was sprung on me but that whole documentary was nearly all set up by people Brian knew. Brian made a cunt of himself on the show as far as I'm concerned.

On the show he told Donal he tied a lad up at the Gare in Redcar, well "ODIN ODIN TURN BACK THE TIDE". He must have been watching too much of the fucking Vikings film with Kirk Douglas and Tony Curtis in the silly cunt.

Brian was my big pal and I loved him, but from what I knew he had fallen in love with a nasty little habit called crack cocaine and he was busy ruining his life in my opinion.

Me and Brian got some big money in, but he ruined himself on that shit. I don't say this to stab him in the back, I'm putting it, so it encourages him to get off the shit! Even now he's not what he once was, I don't know a man in this town who'd go toe to toe with Cockerill the size he is. He'd still be too much for anyone in Middlesbrough that's for sure.

Brian's uncle is Frank McGivern who once played for Manchester United and he's a great fellow. To talk to him you wouldn't even know he played for Man Utd because he doesn't bring it up and is totally the opposite to Brian. I've had many tremendous nights out with Frank in Redcar and I must go see him again soon, lovely man.

Brian today, I don't know about him or what he's up to, but I wish him well I hold no malice, but I don't see us ever being friends again. I wish him all the happiness in the world, but he's got no chance of being the man he once was while smoking that shit. He also shit on me and I was the most loyal friend he ever had. Friendship and loyalty mean everything to me, it's just a shame Brian doesn't have the same morals as me. Brian is very much like Tommy Harrison and he's living in his own little world. Brian Cockerill if you're in his company is only ever interested in himself BIG BRI BIG BRI BIG BRI.

Brian once told me he had the IQ the same as Albert Einstein. I asked him "Brian if your IQ is so high what the fuck you doing using crack cocaine young Albert?" Now we all know the theory of gravity, but it must have been more than a fucking apple that fell on his head! I also know the theory of liars and he's one lying bastard. When you lie to make yourself look good you're only kidding yourself young Albert.

Although I've had my say about Brian, and it does anger me to think that he double crossed me, please don't take that as a sign of his weakness, as he is still a big powerful man and cross him at your peril.

"Friendship and loyalty can't be bought."

8

Snakes & Ladders

Tommy Harrison is a name I first came across when he was having trouble with Davey Bishop over the border in the early 70's. Now Tommy is 15 years older than me but at the time I was just a kid firing my pellet gun at him as he was fighting with Davey. I don't know why because I didn't know him, but I just kept taking aim at Tommy aiming for his head, I don't know if I got him or not that day as in all the years we were friends I never asked him about it. To be truthful I can't even remember who won the fight, but I know Davey knocked Tommy on his arse. I myself ended up in Durham prison with Tommy in 1980.

I was friends with Tommy Harrison for maybe thirty odd years and once over we were very close, and he was the most connected man I knew. Tommy introduced me to the likes of Freddie Foreman among many others of the same genre.

I always knew of Tommy's reputation, he wasn't to be trusted and I knew he wasn't well liked on Teesside. Yes, he was a rough man, an ex-professional boxer and he could have a fight, but I never ever saw him fight apart from the day I was shooting him with my air rifle as a kid.

Tommy Harrison has a loyal best friend named John "Buster" Atkinson who's been his right-hand man for almost 50 years, everyone in Middlesbrough knows how loyal Buster has been to Tommy and how close they were but I personally think, as a good friend of Busters myself, that Tommy has treated Buster disgustingly all the way through their friendship. Buster's done prison for Tommy a few times and he's even turned on him and got people in jail to hiss at Buster like he was a grass, well I don't know how he fucking dare! I told my son Terry, who was in there at the time, if anyone gives Buster any shit then get stuck into them.

Apparently, the reason Tommy got inmates to hiss at Buster was because Buster went guilty over an incident that was down to Tommy in the first place. Buster had been told by his barrister that if he went not guilty he was going to be given double figures, so he went guilty and received four years. That was only for Tommy Harrison's benefit to begin with, as Buster was covering up Tommy's dirty work linked to his son Lee Harrison and Lee's involvement in the manslaughter of market trader Kalvant Singh in August 2001, for which Lee received a nine-year sentence in 2004 after being apprehended in Jamaica after fleeing the UK following Mr Singh's death. Tommy Harrison received 10 years himself by Judge Peter Fox in 2005 so he was inside with Buster making his life hell for something he dragged him down for in the first place!

*** This is how the Gazette reported on it on 11th February 2005: ***

"The leader of a conspiracy to influence murder trial witnesses and his "principal lieutenant" are behind bars today.

Tommy Harrison, 62, of Ormesby Bank, Middlesbrough, has been jailed for ten years and ordered to pay £23,433 legal costs.

His co-conspirator John 'Buster' Atkinson, 55, of Orchard Way, Ormesby, was jailed for four years at Teesside Crown Court yesterday.

The associates conspired to pervert the course of justice between March 19 and July 1 last year in the then forthcoming trial of Harrison's son Lee, for the killing of market trader Kalvant Singh.

Judge Peter Fox QC branded Harrison an "inherently devious man", arrogantly disdainful of law officers.

Paying tribute to witnesses, he said: "Without people prepared, in the face of adversity at times, to have the courage to speak and to speak the truth, we are lost."

He told the defendants their conspiracy was the most serious of its type - controlled by Harrison with Atkinson as his "principal lieutenant".

They used methods from inducement to threats, property damage, physical violence and coercing one witness to swear a false declaration concocted by Harrison.

The judge rejected submissions that Harrison, found guilty by a jury, was in poor health and had no assets. He said the source of Harrison's wealth "plainly calls for separate investigation".

Atkinson's guilty plea did not indicate remorse, he said, adding: "When you are not wielding Thomas Harrison's authority, you are in my judgment the weak individual, and have long been under his domination."

Father-of-six Mr Singh, 41, was pushed through the first-floor window of a house on Errol Street, Middlesbrough, on August 6, 2001.

Prosecutor Nicholas Campbell QC said Lee Harrison - identified as part of the gang on the "night of violence" - was later traced to Jamaica.

Potential witnesses Rowena Frost and Michael Moody, who was badly injured the night Mr Singh was killed, were approached. Atkinson paid more than £700 for Mr Moody to stay at the Longland's Hotel.

Documents found at Harrison's home seemed to change Mr Moody's statement to deny the presence of Lee Harrison, who later admitted manslaughter and wounding and was jailed for nine years.

Thomas Petch and George Coleman received life sentences for murder, Jonathan Crossling 14 years for manslaughter."

Not many people will know this, but Tommy Harrison told me he had assaulted Judge Peter Fox in Kevin Kelly's house about forty plus years ago at a party, so Judge Fox got his revenge in the end and that's why he gave Tommy ten years I think, he was only getting his own back on Tommy. Peter Fox had a good memory alright. He knew he went overboard with that ten-year sentence, but he didn't care because he held a grudge all that time. Judge Fox told Tommy Harrison he was "An inherently devious man arrogantly disdainful of law officers who's had a hold of the town of Middlesbrough for the last 30 years". He then said to Buster "I'm going give you something to get away from Tommy Harrison" and gave him four years for being Tommy's 'principal lieutenant' under Tommy's long domination. In the end Tommy appealed and got his sentence reduced to 6 years.

Buster has been his driver/runabout for many years because he's loyal and has a good heart to a fault but now I've told him to get away from him, I just hope he sees sense.

I think a lot of people know mine and Tommy Harrison's friendship fell apart in 2015 because I found him out to be one treacherous man. I'll tell you what happened, and it was really nothing to do with me, but he asked me if I'd have a run out in his car with him. As I got in his car on the passenger seat there was a parcel with a large amount of money in it and straight away he's flung it at me. Now when anyone gets something flung at them their immediate reaction is to put their hands up to catch it, so I did. Anyway, as soon as I caught it I realised what he'd done, I've thought you scheming dirty bastard! What he wanted was for my finger prints to be all over the parcel in case we were to get pulled on the way to where we were going.

Towards the end of our friendship Tommy insulted me too many times and I've heard all the stories over the years and I can see they're now true whereas once I wouldn't listen to them because I was fiercely loyal to Tommy Harrison.

Nowadays I'm not sure Tommy's in the best of health but I don't wish him harm. He needs to stop coming up with his hair brain schemes and to stop getting my friend Buster into trouble. He's stolen enough of his life already. Tommy even used to ask me and his oldest friend Buster to swear on the bible that we hadn't ripped him off in certain deals well what a fucking cheek, that was a slap in the face to both of us the cheeky bastard. I would never do that I'm loyal and the last time Buster swore on the bible he was given four years, so I don't know how much weight that would have held anyway.

I spent four days clearing Tommy's house out when he moved from Orchard Way. I feel sorry for Tommy at times I do because he's not earning the money he once was, but you've got to ask yourself how much of Tommy's situation is down to the powers of karma?

In reality Tommy has been conned for years buy some of his Arab friends to invest money in diamonds, gold, power plants, hospitals and more recently there was a project to put his money in railway lines in Iran... Yeah ok, CHOO CHOO Thomas wake up!

I've heard over the last three years that Tommy's said he's going to have me 'whacked' ooh Tommy please don't have me "whacked", well Tommy you know where I drink most nights so make sure you get somebody sufficient to follow out the contract because if I don't go I'm coming to take you with me.

Brian Cockerill once told me that him and Chino were in Tommy's house and Tommy being the ever-boastful man (I prefer Walter Mitty) was on the phone and they could both hear Tommy saying, "Deposit that 1.4 million in that account". Anyway, when Tommy went upstairs Brian dialled the last number and the number Tommy had rang was the talking clock!

Many years ago, I was in the old Speak Easy and Kevin Duckling punched Mick Carey for nothing and he went deaf in one ear and still is to this day. Now when I went to pick Mick up off the floor somebody punched me in the back of the head and I went down. Years later young Billy Price told me "Dicko it was Tommy Harrison that punched you". Now that might not be so out of the question because we were all rough lads living in a rough place doing crazy things, but the best thing about that was that I was out that night with Tommy Harrison and I was his friend. To this day Tommy Harrison doesn't know I know that so he's nothing but a low life bastard and has been all of his life. He likes to play the big man, but he's finished in this town. He's a has-been and finished well and truly. He owes money to people all over Middlesbrough and that's why he doesn't step foot in the town anymore. The snake pawned Buster's Rolex which was lost because he never paid the debt back on time. This fool tells anyone who will listen that he has million-pound deals but in truth he hasn't got a bean. The man has a name worse than shit in Teesside. Tommy even tries to dress like an old gangster, but his suits are outdated by thirty years.

Tommy was the one who sneaked in Barry Faulkner's club like a thief in the night and hit the unsuspected Barry in the legs with a hammer, Tommy had been harassing him for years.

"Always go out of your way for your friends."

9

Middlesbrough Faces

Middlesbrough breeds tough men because it's a hard place to live in any generation. Sometimes, just because you're a hard man doesn't mean you're not a decent man.

One thing I'd like to say, and I feel this deserves a mention in my book, is that when my brother in law died a few years back, apparently, he owed Davey Allo a few quid. As soon as the funeral was out the way I messaged Davey and I told him that I'd now take the debt on myself and I was going to repay him. Davey very decently told me he didn't want it. What I should do is give it to his wife and kids which I thought was a very decent thing for him to do. I spoke to him again a month after and he told me the same and said the debt was dead. He didn't have to do that because it was a lot of money, but I can only commend David for that. Nothing can change what happened between him and Lee Duffy, but I know my friend Lee would have forgiven him. It's now a part of history in Middlesbrough and it will be still be spoken of for many years to come.

Another hard man from the past in Middlesbrough was Kevin Auer from Thorntree. He's sadly been gone twenty years this year and I thought Kevin was a lovely nice polite lad. My first memories of Kevin were when I used to see him about in Rumours nightclub. I saw Kevin fighting Harris from Stockton underneath the arches near Blaises nightclub. Harris was 6ft plus and Kevin was only a small lad like me, but Kevin got the better of him. To look at Kevin you would never have thought he was a fighter, he was also softly spoken, but he was one tough fucker who wouldn't back down from anyone.

A lot of the time people think that you have to be a big powerful man to be a hard man but that's not always the case some of the most dangerous men I have known have been small in stature, but with hearts the size of lions, just like myself.

Another good friend of mine was notorious gunman Keith McQuade from the early 70s. We used to drink in the Erimus (became Rumpoles) and one guy started being funny with me when I was with Keith. This guy was saying that I'd knocked him off his bike 7 years previously. I didn't have the foggiest who he was and even to this day I'm convinced he had me mixed up with somebody else. Anyway, this guy was persistent in picking a fight with me because I was the smallest out of the crowd I was with. I told the lad to forget it, but he told me to step outside. So, me and him leave the Cleveland centre and we got several streets down and we both started fighting. To cut a long story short, I seen this wall brick waving at me, so I smashed his head in with it and there was claret all over. We both walked back to the pub, I walk in first to meet Keith with not a mark on me, he follows looking like he'd been hit by a truck and the full pub started laughing because he was being the bully who started it all.

Many times, over the years I would meet up with Keith and I must say he earnt the huge rep he had. Let me make one thing clear though, I never knew Keith as a fighter, he was just a lunatic who'd think nothing of coming to shoot you if you put it on him, make no mistake and cross Keith McQuade at your peril.

I don't want to be disrespectful, but Keith wasn't a successful career criminal because he was always doing jail.

If you were in his company you'd soon warm to Keith and it would be impossible to dislike him. Keith used to come in the Steam Packet when he wasn't inside and one night I had this kid over from Hartlepool called Calvin Young, so I introduced them both. Anyway, after Calvin walks off I said to Keith "You'll never guess who he works for? He's the bloke who drops the money off from A to B on the security vans. As soon as I'd told Keith that he spat his drink out and he was like "ERE MATE LET ME BUY YOU A DRINK!" Keith's eyes lit up like a Christmas tree.

All the characters of yesteryear in Middlesbrough are a dying breed now. Balla Davies, Franky McKenna and Big Henry Nettleton are all names from yesteryear linked to the town. Big Henry was a big rough man who didn't gave a fuck for anyone and he was my old man's pal right from being young lads. Henry wore a big overcoat, dark glasses and had grey hair and he'd fight anyone. Henry was tragically killed coming home from the pub one night by a motorbike. Years later Henry's daughter Lynn had a son Craig Nettleton. Craig is very much like me with a 'don't give a fuck' attitude and we've become the best of friends.

Billy Terry was another very well-known man in the town and he taught Kev Ducko a lesson or two in the old Wellington playing dominoes. Billy was an ex-boxer but a real shark at playing dominoes. Now Ducko was a bit shark himself for cards and dominoes but Billy had Ducko over a few times in the Clarence club (Dickens Inn). I believe Many years ago you could walk into a bar in the Boro and they'd be all big rough men drinking, well it's very different now to back in the 80s. Middlesbrough pub life was totally different and I think that's a great shame.

Dickie Robbo was another legendary hard man who was always seen in Middlesbrough pubs. Dickie once saved me when I was a little boy climbing for pigeons. He climbed up the building drunk as a cunt and he carried me down. The legendary JP Jackie Parsons (who was a relation of the author) and Maca Harding were real faces in Middlesbrough also.

Over the years many people i.e. Scotch, Irish, Welsh have come to the town for work in the steelworks. That's the reason why Middlesbrough has a massive Irish catholic community and South Bank in particularly.

Over the border you'd get some rough men like Jackie Stevo, Jimmy Ward just to name a couple but most of them have gone now.

One man I would like to give a huge mention to is Gram Seed. Now I used to stumble across Gram over the border and he would usually be begging. Big Gram was a hopeless likeable drunk in the 80's until the mid 90s. Many times, I would see big Gram on the bench outside a Middlesbrough church and he was always blind drunk, he didn't know what day it was, and I would give him a few quid.

Now today Gram has done wonders and changed his life around with the help of Jesus.

Back in November 1996 he was going nowhere, in fact he was given the last rites and a group of Christians visited him and came to pray around his unconscious body in the hospital. I truly believe that day Gram was saved by the power of god who brought him back to life.

Gram is a testament and it puts a chill through me when you think of how he was, to how he is today. He's no longer the drunken, useless waster and down and out, I don't mean to sound horrible to Gram there but that's what he was. Now gods turned his life around and he's not the no hoper anymore, what he is, is hope on legs and I absolutely applaud him. He fills me full of hope for my own journey in life.

Gram spends his time going into prison to help stop these young kids from ruining their lives and delivers to them the messages of Jesus himself.

One man who I think deserves a mention was little John Pearce Senior. Now little JP was an original Cannon Park lad and was one hell of a featherweight back through the 60s. He had a left hook like train for such a little man and his son John Pearce Junior was a real boxing legend winning the ABA'S twice. John Junior also won the 1998 Commonwealth Gold at Kuala Lumpur.

It was John Senior who labelled me "The Gremlin" about thirty years ago. I hadn't seen John Senior for many years until around 2012 when I went to Keith Nettleton's (Netsa) funeral. It was Peter Powell who I saw in the Brambles Farm pub and when I asked him if he'd seen anything of little John Senior? He said, "Yes of course he's in the bar, come and have a word with him". So, as I went in the bar and Peter said to John "Look who I've found!" John Senior turned and looked at me in sheer terror and even put his hands up in fear shouting "OOOOH IT'S THE GREMLIN". I gave John a hug, he's a lovely guy.

Freddie Vasey was a man in Middlesbrough in who I greatly admired. Freddie ran several nightclubs in our town such as The Belmont, Blinkers and The Speak Easy. Freddie got all sorts in his clubs and what I really liked about Fred was that he wouldn't put up with any crap from anyone. He'd point his finger at people in the foyer and tell them straight. Not only did Freddie run nightclubs but he was a real wheeler-dealer often selling watches, rings, chains etc... Freddie has now sadly passed like many of my old friends.

I think one of the most notorious of all characters from Middlesbrough was Ronnie Keogh, or as he was better-known Keogh the tramp. Now Ronnie was just another large drunken figure but very entertaining and articulate with it. He'd literally come out with all sorts and be telling the masses of people standing around him that he once went on a date with the Queen or if he was in the magistrates he'd tell the judge to get a move on because he was playing golf with the chief constable in the afternoon. Not many people will know that Ronnie Keogh was an extremely highly educated man but towards the end of his life he became a drunkard and would often beg people for a drink.

When I was in Durham prison I was in there with Ronnie and I looked through the spy hole of his cell and what I'd seen blew me away. He'd drawn an oil painting of Prince Charles and you'd have thought a professional had done it. I don't think old Ronnie was a career criminal or even a fighter for that matter, but he was always causing bother around the town and I dare say he had his own cell down the old Middlesbrough police station. I don't think Ronnie caused anybody any harm he was just a harmless drunk and very well known in our town throughout the 80s. He would sit outside The Masham and he'd make his own stories up and that man entertained an awful lot of people in Middlesbrough on a daily basis.

As I've said Middlesbrough was full of characters many years ago and these days you can't even go in the pub and have a joke on as I myself have been told off a few times for a bit of harmless banter, stuff like pulling peoples trousers down etc... Nowadays the boozers in the town are far more interested in serving people coffee than the old traditional pint. It's just not the same drink culture anymore in Middlesbrough and the diversity has changed so much. Saying that, the town has gotten so much bigger whereas you'd just have near the Welly back in the old days it's right up near Southfield Road and right up towards Linthorpe Road now as its mainly concentrated on the students.

Another real character from over the border was "Blind Frankie". Now Frankie was a character and a half and couldn't see, cataracts I believe. Most days I would see him stood near The Fleece and I'd say, "Come on Frankie I'll walk you over the road and into the pub" and he'd link me to The Ship Inn. Frankie would be in the pub and I'd sneak up and flick his lugs or rub his leg and he'd scream in laughter "DICKO STOP FUCKING ABOUT".

One of the funniest stories of Frankie was when Kenny Graham, Arthur 'Odd Boot' Hayes and a few other border lads took him to see Middlesbrough F.C away to Millwall and as they were all sat facing the football pitch they faced Frankie, all the way through the game, facing the Millwall fans. Obviously, Frankie being blind wouldn't have had a clue but the Millwall fans thought Frankie was looking over at them for chew for 90 minutes at them. I know people might think that's cruel but Kenny Graham and all the lads there looking after Frankie that day fucking loved him and looked after him, he was part of the furniture on the Boro away bus. Frankie was a border lad and one of us, but he could give it back as much as we used to wind him up.

Sid and Podgie Forman are both good border lads. In fact, it was Sid who I bought the Packet off and put it under a travelling man's name. When the police went to see him they asked him if he'd been in the Packet lately? Sid said of course I have. The copper said, "It's that nice I'd take my wife in there".

"I am a violent man who has learned not to be violent and regrets his violence". John Lennon

10

If I had a Hammer

In July 1991 my 8 year old son was left for dead. A week later I was locked up and charged with kidnap and assault and spent a week inside prison. I can't even really go into specific details about the case as it's an ongoing case with Cleveland police at this very minute. The reason I want to add this in the book is because this is a prime example of me standing up for my family, like any good parent would but the authorities have used incidents like this to say that I'm an incredibly dangerous man. When, in reality, I did what any sane thinking man would have done if he'd have been in the same situation.

I'm not going to let you all believe I haven't done anything wrong because I have and I'm not a fucking liar! Yes, at times in my life the violence excited me, and I had a switch which I flicked when it was required. Sometimes I even enjoyed the acts of violence that were dished out, but it was never to any innocent parties.

My thinking was, when people tried to put it on me, that I was going to make them wished they'd never. Quite often in situations I know I've been picked on because I was small by maybe certain doormen etc in the town. Nearly always they've come away thinking "Fuck going near that nasty little bastard again". I was like a Honey Badger when provoked but I've never put it on anyone who didn't deserve it. Hand on my heart and on my children's lives I've never went out in the town of Middlesbrough and committed acts of violence for kicks. Anyone drinking in a pub minding their own business never had anything to worry about from me ever. I'm just too polite and if I was to see anyone getting bullied I'd always be the first man in the bar to jump up and break it up.

I've always had compassion in my life and even God, although that might surprise some people. The first thing I do when I've done something wrong is say "God forgive me!"

As I said at the start of my book my Mother and Father always ingrained it in me as a kid to go out of your way and help people and I still carry them morals today. I've always loved helping people of the community but in today's society it's greatly lacking. That's what I loved about being brought up in a place over the border, it always had a marvellous community spirit which you'd be pushed to find anywhere in Middlesbrough today.

Going back to the violence, I know that I've been told that many people in Middlesbrough see me as a figure of evil and that I revelled in the violence, but I'd like to make it clear once more that I never ever started it. Yes, I'm a firm believer that if somebody wants to hurt me I make sure I fucking hurt them but that's how you should be. To stick up for yourself and see what's right as I will continue to do so till I'm in the grave.

As you'll be aware now in this book I have had to use extreme violence when necessary, although at times my temper has snapped with people and I've stuck one in people's legs like a warning from a rattle snake. There's been so many times though I've been chewed by big men before I've reacted like that. I've had to do wicked things like that when people have walked into the bar and tried to embarrass me and chew me when I've been in people's company, I just wouldn't allow it. I always gave these people a lot of warning but some people, when their full of drink and drugs, won't be deterred. I've had guys in pubs coming up to me trying to demand money from me and that's why I've went "ERE FUCK OFF" and probably put an ashtray over their heads.

God forgive me for saying this, but I've probably lost count of the pricks that I've had to stick one in their legs, but my world was and is a dirty horrible world. In the Packet most weekends it was the only code some people respected.

One day one of my very good friends Lee 'Oathead' Owens, the notorious football hooligan from Stockton, came over to The Ship Inn and asked, "Is Terry Dicko here?" But I'd just left. So, he came over to the Steam Packet looking for me for a night out. I was great mates with Lee but at the time he brought a squad from Stockton and before he came in he warned them "Do not fuck about in here because Terry's a psychopath!" So, there must have been about eight of them walked in and within minutes there was blood everywhere, a lad had been injured so I went up and said, "Who's done that to you son?" The lad told me it didn't matter but this kid who was with Oathead, a little shit who's not even worthy of a mention in this book, but he was a little bully from Hardwick butted in and said, "Listen to him it doesn't matter!" So now it became clear to me this was the culprit. I told him there and then if any more of it went on I'd be coming for him! I knew as soon as I clocked him he was a right cheeky cunt and he took my hospitality by buying him a drink as a weakness, well that was the biggest mistake of his life because he hit the poor lad again in front of me. Straight away I locked the door and the barmaid handed me a hammer and I went to town on him and I enjoyed it. My friends who were there then started fighting with the Stockton lot so I had to pause my hammering (breaks out into singing the hymn 'If I had a hammer') and stop Oathead from fighting with young John Howard etc... Outside the lad started mouthing at me again as I was trying to get him a lift from the Steam Packet resident taxi driver Buster, so I ran out and started hammering him again all over. Buster dragged me off him in the end and he spent three days in hospital, but he was a vile bully he got what he deserved and if I was asked I'd say I don't regret that happening and I'd do the same thing again.

Months later I was in Stockton having a night out with my Mrs when I saw big Tommy Oliver and we were chatting away. I don't know how we got on the subject, but I asked him if he ever went to the Packet in Middlesbrough? His reply was a very funny one, he said

"Fuck that, my mates went once, and they got locked in and brayed with hammers". He didn't even know I had the Steam Packet.

When I was young I was probably guilty of producing too much testosterone!

There was an incident in The Wellington public house. A lad sat in my seat and I just politely told him he was sat in my seat and did he mind moving? He then blatantly told me to "FUCK OFF!" I could have lived with it if he hadn't of shown me up the way he did, so what I did was I went and got a samurai sword from my brothers flat in Exchange Place, which was over the road, and I came back and started chasing him around the pub and he done a runner. Looking back, I was too crazy and too wild, but he put it on me in front of the whole pub and I wasn't having it.

It's only when I look back at 61 years old today with hindsight that it's truly amazing I'm not doing a life sentence.

I know I've done things wrong in my life and I'll be the first to admit that. There were times in the Packet I caught men dealing drugs and I've turned on them when looking back I probably shouldn't have. Maybe that was a bit hypercritical because the place was full of drugs! I caught one lad in the toilets with a load of stuff, but I told the doormen not to hurt him. Funny enough I became good friends with this traveller lad years later but at the time I wasn't best pleased that he was taking the piss, so I took his money off him and flung the tablets down the toilet. The sum of money I took off him was £80 but me being the decent guy gave him £20 for his taxi home but warned him not to come back again. Years later he mentioned it to other travelling friends saying I was a good lad and I had stopped him getting a kicking from the bouncers. He could have been severely hurt especially coming somewhere like that, but I didn't want that. I don't like to see people hurt if it can be helped. Then again sometimes in life people need to be taught a lesson.

It's not only that, I've been around violence most of my life. I've seen the Brian Cockerill's, Lee Duffy's and Kevin Auer's of this world going to war.

Middlesbrough has and always will be a very rough place to live and of course boys will be boys. Look I was brought up in a rough dockland area and it was survival of the fittest. We were brought up over the border, so I was condemned all my life and maybe I had a chip on my shoulder.

One name the people from St Hilda's had to endure was the name 'border rats' and I believe that term was brought about by Joe Livo who called one of the Woodier's it whilst they were fighting one time. It's a name unworthy of border lads and unworthy of the community. I loved the place and we all stuck together and had a great time being brought up over there. I'm just sad it's all gone now.

If you couldn't fight you didn't survive I'm afraid, so I have had to have a mental toughness in life. Maybe I'm a product of coming from the approved schools, it was certainly no fun getting battered in remand centres and getting battered in Medomsley D.C and that's why I've always hated authority of any kind or bullies putting it on me. Yes, there's been times I've come unstuck, been knocked out cold and endured beatings, but the first thing on my mind has been revenge. Revenge has always been very important to me and it still is today. Nobody wronged me and ever got away with it, even if it took a week, month or a year I always got my pound of flesh.

One of these cases was with a very good friend of mine so I won't mention his name, but he put it on me terribly and I was knocked out and took away in an ambulance. I don't remember much of what happened, but I was hit that hard that I was out before I hit the floor, I hit my head on the pavement and I sustained an horrendous cut. I was covered in claret and the people around thought I was dead. Anyway, I was taken off and stitched up and the first thing I did hours later was to go home, get a different shirt on and straight back out looking for revenge. The lad who was the brother of the fella that had walloped me said to him "What did I tell you, Dicko's out of hospital and he's out looking for you". In the end nothing happened because of it and I'll tell you, the reason why is that when I'd sobered up I realised I was bang out of order in the first place. I knew I was in the wrong, so I went and apologised, and he was in the right to put it on me. I'd insulted him. In fact, fuck it, it was Kenny Howard who the war was with, Kenny's a good lad and I have great respect for him and we're friends. All the Howards are my friends. Looking back, it would have been easier to continue to proceed with war because it's very difficult to say sorry. It takes a real man to hold his hands up and apologise.

It doesn't mean I've always liked to see it, violence is ugly, but it is better in this world if it doesn't put the fear of god into you at certain times. We don't live in an ideal world in the 21st century unfortunately. There were certain times I haven't had to do it, but I've instigated it from other people when I was doing the debt collecting but at the same time I did it in a polite manner.

Over the years I've been asked many times to be the mediator with people in Middlesbrough who've had their clashes. Friends who I know from either side have come to me and asked me to arrange meetings, so things can be sorted out, so the least possible amount of blood has been shared. I have done that on many, many occasions and I've always got a wage out of it as well, although that was never my motive if it was between my friends. I get asked because I'm very well known in our town and I'm always true and fair. Normally both parties have been happy with my end results although certain times between particular families in Middlesbrough it's been beyond that to the point of no return, but that's Middlesbrough for you.

These days I don't need to get involved in fights, not at 61, besides I'm too quick with the tongue. I'm a charmer I can joke my way out of situations these days. At my age there's no need for violence and I've got nothing to prove, but if you're reading this that doesn't mean you can come and put it on me! (laughs).

I've always likened myself to an electric station, don't enter because you'll get a shock! It doesn't matter if your 6ft 8 because when I get half a brick in my hand I'm just as big as you. That was my attitude then but not now. Sometimes people wronged me though and apologised and I would let it go. I wasn't above reasoning but years ago I was one little bastard.

Me and violence these days are now done although I can never say never. If someone cornered me I'd stand my ground, I wouldn't give a fuck for the consequences and I'll still be like that when I'm in my 80's if god spares me. My Dad was the same.

As I've said through this book many times I'm not the biggest man, but my bottle is unquestionable and bigger than most men's. If anyone was to ever stab me up or take a hammer to me I would never run to the police. But believe me and let god be my witness, you'd better fucking finish me whilst you're there because I will not let it go and I'll come back!

What I like about life is being loyal to people. My loyalty is unquestionable to any of my friends in Teesside. Nobody in Middlesbrough could ever say Terry Dicko's failed him or let him down on purpose. Loyalty means more to me than money ever did and that's why my friendship with Cockerill fell apart. Even my friends who've gone like Lee Duffy, Mick Rooney, Paul 'Minty'

Marlowe, Kev and Leo Auer, I still speak about them all the time and they will always have my loyalty.

When I think of the whole of Middlesbrough I can't think of many people who I don't know or don't know me.

I suppose if I'm being truthful with myself I've always had that aggressive nature and a spark of madness about me. I was never like Ronnie Kray though who went out and carried out acts of wickedness, but once somebody provoked me it wasn't getting left.

At times I'm sure I've had bouts of mental illness where I've been on my knees and really questioned my own sanity and whether my life was worth living, but it's like Winston Churchill said, "If you're going through hell keep going" and I've got through the shit. Besides, I wouldn't give the Middlesbrough police the satisfaction of me topping myself! So, when I've been low I've stayed on this planet just to spite them.

"If someone puts their hands on you make sure they
never put their hands on anybody else again".
Malcolm 'X'

11

You don't have to be big to be Dangerous

To describe myself as not being Cleveland police's favourite person is like describing Adolf Hitler as being "a little naughty". When I was growing up over the border it was brayed into you that the old bill was the enemy and you mustn't ever help them with their enquiries.

As a child I was suspicious of any kind of authority anyway. When I was a kid me and my mates would have our own special kind of whistle if we ever saw them to warn others. It was a certain style of whistle and one night we heard it and turned around and there were two coppers using it (without permission I might add) they'd got wise to our way.

Two years ago, I was in the Longlands W.M.C when there was two of the main police sergeants in there playing pool. I was in there with my mate Danny Blackley. I walked up to them and said, "Hello lads how are ya?" Immediately I could tell both were very standoffish as if they were wondering 'what's he about to fucking do to us this loon'. Now although I've been seriously harassed from the police, these two were out

111

of uniform and I wouldn't dream of being disrespectful to either of them. At the end of the day they're just doing their job. I'm the 'bad un' who's been up to things in life at times and I see a line of respect towards them in that sense. It's just cops and robbers isn't it and they're the cops and can you guess which one I am? Both have always gone hand in hand like fish and chips, salt and pepper and cats and dogs.

What I'd like to point out in this book is yes, I've done wrong with the law, but there's been police officers who really went out of their way to get me when I haven't even been doing anything. I've had crimes committed against me by nothing other than bent coppers is how I can only describe it. When I was "at it" doing the Steam Packet I could take what they were doing to me on the chin, I was running an illegal nightclub for god sake, so I knew I was bringing something like that on myself. What I can't get my head around is officers driving past my girlfriend and calling her a 'slag' just so she comes back to me and tells me, because they know it will wind me up. Well I was fucking outraged, as you can imagine, so I went to the senior DCI and demanded to know who it was! I said not only is she my girlfriend, but she's also the niece of Ken Walker who's the chairman of the police authority. To cut a long story short I managed to track both down at Middlesbrough police station and told them to come and do it to me! They said, "You think you're something you Dicko!" I told them "I'm here on my own and what you did was fucking disgusting you pair of shithouses". I know they were spoken to on their actions that day because I'd never let it go.

I would take satisfaction when they sent the mufti squad out with all the officers dressed in riot gear to the Steam Packet when I was never there. I had a friend whose Wife was a copper and he'd tip me off at times and tell me about the raids before they even happened, so I'd keep away. Sometimes I'd move the party to another place and I'd leave a note on the door for them saying "If I knew you were coming I'd have baked a cake".

The police used to send spies into the Steam Packet on a regular basis, but I would always sniff them out. They came in one day, four of them, and they moved a table in there, so they could have a camera put in place with a better view.

One thing I always did in the Packet was I'd be seen to put my hand in my pocket and pay for my drink. One day I was sat down with a spy he let the cat out of the bag by saying to me "Nice place you've got here mate!" I said to him "It's not my place". He said "Yes, it is, yes, it is!" I said "Excuse me but when did I ever tell you this was my place echo tango?" Then I walked up to the doorman Lee Little and said get rid of him for his own safety.

I've seen letters on police intelligence that Cleveland police have me down for murdering people and burying the bodies. Can I just say now that I've never killed anyone. Yes, we've all said things in anger like "Ooh I'm gonna kill you" but I've never physically tried to kill anyone. I'm not a drug dealer but the police say otherwise. They have me down for kidnaps when in truth I've made a citizen's arrest on one man in my life.

The police know me for having once been closely associated with Middlesbrough's Tommy Harrison. Now I always knew Tommy had a bad name but I became friends with him and I overlooked that but that was a major mistake on my part. Even my traveller friends used to say, "What you doing knocking about with him?" but I was too easy going. I now know he brought me a lot of police attention that wouldn't have been there otherwise.

Like I said I've never buried any bodies, but if anyone wants their garden turning over and doing please give me a shout. No, jokes aside, I've inflicted some serious harm on people but only people who were trying to do the same to me.

Luckily, I've always been able to come out on top. Yes, I've lost fights and I'm only a little lad, but I just won't let stuff go and I always come back, always!

At times my own solicitors have said to me, "Terry you must be involved with something why do the police treat you so badly?" I've had this fight with the police 27 years since a date I won't go into which had a huge impact on my life.

One officer did say to me once that from all the stories he'd heard about me he expected me to be 6ft plus. He'd been looking for me for driving offences and he asked one copper then another copper where could he find Terry Dicko? One said try 9 West Street, the other said 1 Vine Street. It turned out that I was in the cells. The policeman jumped down the stairs and opened my cell door he had a strange bewildered look on his face. That's when he said I thought you'd be a lot bigger than you are from all the stories I'd heard about you!

I replied, "My philosophy in life is you don't have to be big to be dangerous!" Many times, the police used to say to me before turning the light off "Goodnight Mr Dixon" To wind me up. I usually replied with "Don't goodnight me" I despise you lot.

I still have ongoing battles with Cleveland police even today, I've been fighting them for 27 years and I'll fight them for another 27 years if need be, although this one is coming to an end and I've won. I sadly can't reveal what it's about just yet for legal reasons.

When I was younger I just didn't give a fuck and that led me to spending many nights at Boro cop shops en suite facility. I've never eaten what they gave me in there though, you don't know what they were going to put in it, especially in my case as I am not exactly their favourite person.

I've been a thorn in their side for a long time. Funnily enough the last time I was checking in at hotel Boro cop shop was this year in 2018. I was in 17 hours, but I was released without charge. Nothing became of it. They even gave me a blanket this time. When I checked in they asked, "Are you on any medication Mr Dixon?" I said, "Only for my schizophrenia", I haven't got schizophrenia although some people might doubt that!!!!

It's funny because I told them "I only moved from over the border when you fuckers moved in" (Middlesbrough police station's newer station is located there) I said, "You were giving my street a bad name".

I've been told on good authority that the police have all kinds of nicknames for me such as 'The Mad Axe-man, little bastard from over the border, Cockerill's pal and many other derogatory names. Me and Cleveland police are like that married couple who are always arguing but are in love with each other. I hope we have many more years together yet. Even though I've had many a struggle with Cleveland police I have had some decent officers who've pulled me to one side and said, "Keep at em it's wrong what they're doing to ya!" I will make sure they're going to be held accountable for what they've done and they're gonna have to kill me to shut me up. I'm not going away.

I'll tell you a really bizarre story, I've been on the same news programme twice in one bulletin! The newsreader said "There has been raids on an illegal nightclub in Middlesbrough today in Cleveland police's efforts to banish illegal drinking establishments" they didn't name me personally of course but we all knew that they were talking about the Steam Packet as they even showed footage of them filming the raids. Then in the Newsreaders next breath they brought Cleveland the news of a really wonderful fella, Terry Dixon, who had been invited to the House of Commons for his community work in and around St Hilda's in Middlesbrough! You couldn't make it up!

"We are each our own devil, and we make this world our Hell". Oscar Wilde

12

A Smashing Day

On February 14th 2012, which is Valentine's Day funnily enough, there was no love lost between me and the Middlesbrough MP Stuart Bell. That was the day I was brought before the magistrates as I pleaded guilty to smashing an egg on Stuart Bell's head following a 20-year dispute between us. I did what I did to Stuart to publicly shame and embarrass him because I asked him for help for a case which I've been fighting for 27 years now.

Now Stuart wrote a book on Middlesbrough and stood up to represent people like myself in the houses of parliament, yet my cries of help fell on his deaf ears.

I've been in a queue stood waiting for a chance to speak with Mr Bell and when it's been my turn to speak with him amicably he refused to speak with me which is an outright disgrace! His job is to be there for the people and even though I phoned his office over a hundred times, he didn't do anything.

Stuart Bell likes to come across like a champion of the people, but he shied away when I was asking for his help. I found the man a hypocrite and a disgrace to his profession so that's why I did what I did with the egg to shame him. He did nothing for me and my family when we begged for his help and I'm still to this day extremely upset and don't understand it.

Today I have a banning order which means that I can't go anywhere near Mr Bell's home or approach his Wife, Lady Bell. Can I just say now, I have no intention of approaching his home or his Wife at all.

Today I'd like to say god bless Stuart Bell, his Wife and his family but he did nothing for my family when in reality he was the man in power.

I did what I did for a reason and I'm glad I did it because somebody else has since come forward and is now helping me in my case. Let me just say I did what I did to Stuart because I wanted to humiliate him. It wasn't about the violence but if I had one regret over doing it I should have used a bag of flower and not the egg to shame him more.

In court I received £175 fine and a lovely lady, who's a fellow counsellor of Beechwood & Easterside called Joan McTigue even offered to pay the full fine because she could see my cries of help went unanswered. Now that was very kind of Joan to offer that but I'm old fashioned and I believe it's a man's place to sort his own fines out but thank you Joan it was very kind of you to offer.

The incident of me egging Mr Bell was captured on a camera phone and posted on YouTube which has since had thousands of views although it's since been removed from the site. Even in court my solicitor John Nixon said that I'd done it through many years of being failed and that I felt a huge injustice over an incident which left my 8 year old son for dead in an alleyway in 1991.

Speaking outside of court to the papers I said, "What do I have to do to get justice for my son?" I suffer post-traumatic stress. As soon as I go to bed and it gets dark, that is when the nightmares begin, it has never left me for 20 years. I have hit him on the head to draw attention to my plight. I know it was wrong and I should not have done it, but what do I have to do to get justice? If I must, I will hang a banner from the Transporter Bridge to draw attention to what happened.

Sir Stuart declined to comment on the case, saying he'd already made a statement to the court that he no longer holds open surgeries because I had been harassing him for 20 years.

Well I was just wanting what was right for my family and I'll continue to fight for that until my last day on this earth.

*** Article from the Evening Gazette dated 14th February 2012: ***

A MAN who threw an egg at Sir Stuart Bell MP during a Remembrance Day parade has admitted the assault in court.

Terence Edward Dixon struck the Middlesbrough MP with the egg at the town's cenotaph on Linthorpe Road.

Dixon, 54, of Liverton Avenue, West Lane, Middlesbrough, previously denied the "assault by beating" charge.

He was set to stand trial at Teesside Magistrates' Court yesterday morning but changed his plea to guilty.

The court was told he attacked Sir Stuart out of a feeling of "injustice" on the morning of November 13 last year.

He believed he had not been fully helped in trying to reopen investigations into an attack on his son years ago.

Sir Stuart and his wife Lady Margaret were speaking to Middlesbrough mayor Ray Mallon and several leading Middlesbrough councillors at the end of the service.

Prosecutor Philip Morley said: "He was struck to the back of his head with an egg. He turned to see Mr Dixon who was shouting abuse toward him. Mr Dixon was detained and arrested, and in his interview made full admissions."

It was previously reported that Mr Mallon made a citizen's arrest and held the suspect until police arrived.

John Nixon, defending, said: "Many years ago my client's son sustained horrific injuries in an assault. My client found his son unconscious in a rear alley. A man was convicted of a serious assault upon him. But today my client believes that investigation was not carried out properly or thoroughly.

"There have been repeated requests made by him for certain aspects of the investigation to be further considered and further inquiries to be reopened, the case to be reopened. That has not been done.

"My client contacted Sir Stuart seeking assistance. Unfortunately, my client's perception was that full assistance has not been given. My client's action on this day, the court will view as being misguided, I'm afraid was borne out of a long sense of injustice."

District Judge Kristina Harrison said Sir Stuart was vulnerable as a public figure. She said: "He has to be seen in public in a position of prominence and therefore leaves himself open to possible attacks of this nature."

She said this was an aggravating feature of the assault, but the offence was "certainly not at the top end".

A pre-sentence report will be prepared on Dixon, whose last conviction was in 2005. He will be sentenced for the assault on March 5. The court will be asked to consider a restraining order.

Judge Harrison allowed Dixon conditional bail, under which he is not to approach, contact or communicate with the MP.

Outside court, Dixon said: "I was advised by my solicitor to plead guilty because I did it. I am guilty. I know it was wrong. I shouldn't have done it. But what do I have to do to get justice?

"I'm still jumping up in my sleep, picking up my son from the floor. I suffer post-traumatic stress.

"It's never left me for 20 years. It's frustrating for me. I only want closure. I wouldn't wish this on my worst enemy."

Sir Stuart, who did not attend the court hearing, declined to comment on the case.

"Sometimes the Devil is a gentleman"
Percy Bysshe Shelley

13

The Calming of the Storm

These days I don't do a lot apart from continue my fight with my other half Middlesbrough police station. I've just had a meeting with the Chief Constable who's a very decent man and he's helped me get what I'm entitled to after such a long time fighting.

Terry Dicko today is just a nice polite man who doesn't get into anyone's problems. I'm very passionate about doing my gardening these days and any time I'm not gardening I spend it with my beautiful little Mrs Leslie. My life has changed 100%. I'm not that crazy man anymore. I don't need trouble and I don't want trouble, that part of my life is gone, although it was good while it lasted. (Terry laughs)

Life in 2018 has become a lot better for me now I've got God in my life. The Terry Dixon here today is a different man than the one you may have once known. Years ago, you couldn't look at me if you'd done me wrong. Now I just want peace because I want forgiveness for the things that I myself have done wrong. If I want forgiveness I have to forgive people also, I know that.

I was in The Ship Inn one day when I got talking to this girl. I can't even remember her name, but she was a pretty lass and I was just at the end of the bar contemplating life in general. Now my friend Brian Thompson who owned the pub said, "Ere Terry, meet my friend" and he introduced me to the pretty girl who's name I've since forgotten. Anyway, Brian asked me to shake her hand and he was becoming almost 'parrot like'. So, I asked "Brian, why are you so keen for me to shake this lovely girl's hand?" Anyway, I ended up shaking the lasses hand and Brian was smiling and he said to her "Tell him where you work" then she said she worked as a lab technician which I thought would make her some kind of scientist, then she said "I work in the morgue" and I said "Give me my handshake back" and I went and washed my hands. I came back laughing and I got talking to the lass and I told her my friend was Lee Duffy, she then told me it was her who had looked after Lee while he was in the morgue and that made me really fill up and I became emotional. I was intrigued with what she was telling me, and I'd been sat telling her about my life and she turned around and asked me where had all the anger come from? In that moment when I sat there and self analysed it, I came to the conclusion it was from the approved school, so it was at that moment I decided I should calm down. Here was this girl whose career was to deal with dead bodies and she must have seen all sorts including dead children etc, which must be horrific for anyone. So, it was at that point I told myself that I needed to calm it and I did.

As I said in the start of the book as a child in my gangs I was always the game stand the craziest and I really have no idea why it took until I was in my fifties, but it

126

was that meeting with that lovely lady from the morgue that kick started my chance I would say.

I do have plans in the next five years. A lot depends on my cases I'm fighting with the police, so I can't make concrete plans until the many cases are resolved. I plan on whatever the outcome is to move forward. I'll never get back the 27 years for the battle I've fought but I'll make the remainder of my life better.

I do get out and about though, I've already been away to Ibiza, Istanbul and Tenerife this year.

I also plan on doing a lot more with Leslie next year. Leslie can be an awkward little fucker at times, but I love her and she's the one for me. I've been with Leslie for 10 years and we have a daughter together called Ruby-May who is 8 years old, and although I can't see us getting married, I think she'll be able to get a ring out of me. I mean, I can't get down on one knee for her as I'm 61 and she's 29 so I might not get back up if I even tried. I do love you Leslie. xxx

"My loyalty to my friends is great and unquestionable,
but my desire for revenge is greater".

14

Talking to Jesus

Now people might be shocked when they read Terry Dixon has faith in God. I don't know why people have said I'm the devil, although I've been a bit of a horny bastard in my time. God means everything to me and it's a big issue in my life certainly. When folk say, "Oh there's no God. It's a load of shite", well when you bang yourself the first thing you shout is "OH GOD" or "Jesus help me" etc... Why do people shout that if they don't believe in him?

I went to church for quite a while and the reason I went to church is that I wanted something different in my life. Even as a kid at ten years old I was a keen drawer and the things I used to draw were churches. Yes, I was pigeon daft and I used to draw pigeon's, but churches have always fascinated me from a young age. I just love looking at architecture.

Once in April 1997 Boro were playing Leicester City in the League cup at Wembley and there was a copper there in the Boro crowd who I knew and he said to me "Are you going to the match Terry?" and I told him "I'm not into football and I've just come down with my friends but I'm going around London to look at the architecture".

He nearly spat his pint out, then he said, "FUCK OFF", I said "I am". He couldn't believe I'd travelled over 250 miles to walk around and have a look at buildings and old churches. The bloke couldn't believe it and he said he always thought I was just a thick fucker from over the border.

In cemetery's you see some wonderful masonry work on gravestones. It fascinated me that a little man has done that with his tools to perfection.

I was christened a catholic, but I know God is God and it doesn't matter what religion you are. Always do good deeds for people and always stand up for people's rights. My Mam was a strong Catholic and she used to say, "When you lie god's listening". My old fella was a Protestant and never bothered as much as our Mam did.

For the people who think I'm the horned demon, I suppose I've had the devil on my back for years but I'm a new man. Even when I see some wicked people who've been on my case for the last nine years I say I'm gonna do this and I'm gonna do that in temper, then straight away I say, "God forgive me". Religion is important to me and people who mock it shouldn't. If they haven't got it then that's their choice. I don't drive what I've got down anybody's throats. I believe in God and I believe in carrying out Gods goodness. I'm very happy I've got Jesus Christ our saviour in my life.

"Every saint has a past and every sinner has a future."
Oscar Wilde

15

A Compassionate Man

For anybody reading this who can't fucking stand me and think I deserve an acid bath I'd like to say this, if there's anybody out there I've ever hurt, or I've upset in any way then I'm truly sorry and I mean that from the bottom of my heart. Please come and let me buy you a pint and I'd like to tell you just how sorry I am.

In life we can all hold grudges that can go on for years and it's no good for you to hold on to resentment. Yes, I was one dangerous little bastard, but I wasn't a big lad so at times in acts of violence against big men I've had to do what I've had to do. I do regret a lot of my actions and over the years I've fell out with friends that meant the world to me and they've helped me in my times of need, so it hasn't been nice.

Anybody out there with scars or cuts from me I wish it could have been different. These days when I pray to God I ask him why I did some of the things I used to do, only he knows the reasons why.

If anybody's reading this and I've hurt you or caused you any harm could you please come and have a pint with me. Please let me hold my hands up in the air and ask you to please forgive me. I've always been a believer in saying something if I've got something to say, I'll tell King Kong if needs be, but if I'm in the wrong I'm also the first person to hold my hands up in the air and say sorry.

I don't sleep much anyway, I maybe get four hours broken sleep a night, but I've had sleepless nights for some of the things I've done in my past that I wish I hadn't.

These days at 61 a lot of things do play on my mind because you can't live a life like I have and not have some sort of remorse. It angers me sometimes and I ask myself why I'm feeling depressed thinking of yesteryear but the answer to my question that I'm seeking is I'm a compassionate man.

If I want to search for something to put the blame on, then I'd like to say it was down to the drink, but I know it's me who decided to drink. Drink has led me into a lot of trouble that I've brought on in my life. I've never really been into cocaine like some of my friends. Yes, I've had it, but it was never my God. Coke makes you angry, it makes you dangerous and I didn't need a top up of what I was about! I'm not going to phone Giff Gaff for a £15 top up on some anger please! Then they'd be like "Here you go Terry and there's half a fucking wall brick to go with it, call back later". (Terry laughs)

I don't fear death, absolutely not. The reason why is that I've had umpteen experiences of seeing and feeling ghosts in my life. Many times, we think we're seeing things and we even think our eyes are playing tricks on us and we try to psychologically explain it in our heads, but sometimes there is no other explanation for it other than it being a spirit.

I saw a ghost of an old man once in The Ship Inn. First, I felt him go past me with a gush of wind, then I got my jumper pulled and then I saw this old man, I turned to set the pool balls up and when I looked again this old man had vanished, but it would have been impossible for him to get by me, absolutely impossible. I then ran and checked the men's and ladies toilets, and nobody was in there. I walked back in the pool room and again I got my jumper pulled. It was a baggy jumper, so I turned side to side trying to get whatever it was off me. The barman Peter asked me what the matter was, and I told him I'd just had my jumper pulled and he said, "That's not possible I've just been watching you and nobody was there". Another time it happened again in The Ship Inn on my brother's memorial on the 18th of March, my jumper got pulled. About an hour later I was at the bar and I shouted at Peter for a double Bacardi& coke and I felt somebody patting me on my stomach as if to say you're putting a bit of weight on but nobody at all was there. Many things happened like that to me in that pub like a little dog cuddling into my leg so as I've bobbed down to say hello there's been nothing there. It wasn't just me it happened to in that pub it happened to my ex-partner, she was walking from one room to another when she started screaming and she's wore blind somebody squeezed her hand.

I believe you've got to be open to receive the spirits and I feel that I've always had psychic powers. People have said over the years the Steam Packet was haunted, but I never ever saw anything, although I put the willies up a few people in there and usually they were blonde with big tits. Saying that, people have said I was the scariest thing in there. I used to have a mask on the wall and at Halloween I would dress up and jump out at people who were off their boilers.

I've had many other ghostly things happen to me, I've had my hair pulled in the night and I'm convinced that's my Dad or my Brother, both were jokers, so I know when I leave here and go to heaven I'm going to be meeting up with all of them, my Mother, Father, Brothers and Grandparents. I know when I get there my friend Lee Duffy will be head of the fucking parade waiting for me shouting "NOW THEN NOW THEN YA LITTLE BASTARD".

I don't want to sound morbid, but while we're on about death I have saved two people's lives so that must give me a bit of leeway with the big fella upstairs. Jack Duffy was choking to death from the gas in the caravan. The gas had blown out and by the time I'd got to him I thought it was a black man because he'd changed colour that much. Anyway, I dragged him out with Peter Woodier, who's also sadly passed away now, and we brought Jack back to life. The other fella whose life I saved was Teddy Cobby who'd burgled Northern Tyres and he had a load of tyres in his back garden. One night Teddy got drunk and decided to set fire to some of his

135

stolen tyres. Now Teddy lived out the back of me and as I'm looking over I can see the flickering of flames from my house, I was getting ready to go to the Steam Packet but as I looked over I could see him passed out from the fumes, so I ran over and brought him out the way. He would have been dead if I hadn't have gotten to him. It does make you feel nice because I've saved a life and I'd do the same thing again. I suppose it was me doing back pay for all the bad things I may have done.

"Everything is funny, as long as it's happening to somebody else". Will Rogers

16

Me & Our Peter

Many years ago, I was out on the rob with Robert and Barry Suggett who are dear friends of mine. I often see Barry and greet him "HELLO BARRYYYYYYYYYYYYY" just to wind him up. Anyway, Brian Andrews was doing The Cornerhouse pub out in Middlesbrough on the corner of the train station and was looking for furniture for his pub. Now me and the lads were very much into antiques as I've already said, and we came across what looked like just a large table which turned. I have many friends who are Landlords in Boro that have bought bits and bobs from us and still do to this day. Anyway, the three of us went to see Brian Andrews and we told him we had this unusual turning table. Now Brian's eyes immediately lit up because he'd done The Corner House out in an almost gothic style and this very much fitted in with what he needed. We told him we wanted £480 but I think we settled for £380 if my memory serves me correctly. So, we handed over this 6ft long, 2 foot wide table, it was all worn down the middle, but we got the money which we got a good drink out of, everybody was happy. A night or two later I went in his bar and seen the table up in the bar and it looked marvellous. I couldn't help but laugh and I said, "You know what you've bought Brian don't you?" He said, "Yes a very nice table and just ideal for in this place". Well the smile soon went from his mug when I got on the table and put my hands across my chest while pretending to be 'brown bread'. His face went from a smile to a scowl and he said "YOU DIRTY BASTARDS" we'd only sold him a coffin table.

About an hour later I could see a few of these trendy looking birds all stood around drinking these special snazzy drinks whilst dancing about. I went over, and I said "Having a good evening are we ladies? Well you do know you're drinking off a coffin table for the dead?" Well I'd never seen anyone pick their drinks up so quickly and move away whilst calling me a sick bastard.

Barry Faulkner my good friend is a top pub and club operator and he personally does his places up to the highest standard. I'd say without a doubt he's the best club runner in Teesside. Me and Barry have had some great laughs and Barry's been very good to me over the years.

Now I love Barry, but he has a terrible sense of humour. In fact, you could put him down as the number one shit-stirrer in Teesside, but I mean that in the nicest possible way.

Although Barry and I are good friends and will remain friends, we have fallen out on a few occasions and on one night in particular I was absolutely furious with him, I went up to one of his clubs and chased one of his doormen around with a big butcher's knife and then I went to Barry's house and stuck it in his door. When I phoned Barry he said, "I'm out I'll catch you later" I said,

"Not if I catch you first!" The next day little Barry his son and Graham, a manager of one of Barry's clubs, came to my house asking what the matter was? I told him what was up and what had upset me, they both knew I was in the right and had every reason to be upset.

What I also did was that I went in another of Barry's clubs and I took an axe to his bar and left it in the wall for him to see. Anyway, the ever so resilient Barry came back and wrote next to the axe "Dicko woz ere" and left it in the club and put pictures next to it. I often laugh about that.

Barry has had some of the top DJ'S in the world to his clubs such as Boy George, Paul Oakenfold, Pete Tong etc... Well some of them would sign their names on the wall and I wrote up alongside them "Dicko's back" after he unbarred me, and Barry put next to it "Yes, but for how long?" Barry forgave me, and I forgave him and we're friends again and I often have a pint with him now and again, he's my friend and always will be.

Barry has met most of the world's big stars and dined out with underworld figures such as Charlie Kray and Charlie Richardson.

One funny story was when Barry was out with Rod Stewart and Barry lent Rod his rather expensive white Levi denim jacket which was a limited edition. Now Barry and Rod were having a right good old booze up in his old club The Kirk. At the end of the night Rod and Barry were going for a mixture of top shelves all mixed with blackcurrant. Well I'm not sure if Rod Stewart threw up or spilt a blackcurrant concoction over his jacket but it was completely ruined. Barry's face was a picture but I'm sure Barry had probably pinched that jacket anyway because our Barry was once the best shoplifter in Middlesbrough town. Barry does like his clothes and many years ago paid £1,000 for a pair of jeans that there are only two pairs of in the world. David Beckham had the other.

I also love little Barry his son and Ashley Wem and both always looked after me as well if I ever needed anything for the Packet. Quite often little Barry would just tell me to go look in the cellar of The Theatre nightclub if I needed anything. Well that was like an Aladdin's cave to me full of pub stuff.

Peter was the name of one of my axes, I don't know why I named him Peter I just did, it was the mad fucker who I was at the time I suppose. Now one night Dave Bishop and Geoff Bailey wouldn't let me in the GO-GO club over the border. So, I told them both I was going to get our Peter, little did they know Peter was my axe, so I came back and told them "I've told Peter". Both just laughed at me and said, "What did he say and where is he?" I brought the axe out from behind me and said, "Ask him yourself he's right here" and with that they both ran in the club and I started chopping the door down like Jack in The Shining "HEEEEEEEEERE'S TERRY!"!!!! Well those two weren't shining that night they looked fucking worried as they tried to reason with me from the other side of the door. God bless Geoff Bailey, who's since passed away and Dave Bishop's always been my pal. I think it must have been a full moon that night because for the life of me I can't even remember why I did it.

Milton Spanswick was a big burly bully, we were friends in jail, but he decided that my late brothers' picture in The Ship Inn was to come down from the wall in my local without any reason. I asked him "Why does it bother you Milton?" He gave me a load of chew and for some reason I couldn't go see Peter that day, so I came back with a two foot scaffy bar and as soon as I walked in the bar he pounced on me, but I was too agile for him. We ended up rolling around the floor. I ended up getting a cracking black eye from the fight inside the pub. The fight spilled out onto the street and that's when I done him across the shoulder with the scaffy bar and he went to run back into the pub. Little did he know but the door wouldn't open, and I laid into him until he curled up in the corner. I never wanted to fall out with big Milton, but he thought he could bully me and disrespect my late brothers' picture which was the biggest mistake of his life. After that fight he came at me again and I put a pool cue over his head.

Over the years he's had many more goes at me. Like the time he came looking for me in The Royal Exchange. He told me to get outside and I walked out but what he didn't know was that I had a heavy short glass in my hand and when he was moving about like a boxer outside I hit him on the side of the head with the short glass and he kind of stopped dead and slumped forward holding his head. I told him "You don't have to bow I'm not royalty, now piss off to the hospital and get stitched up".

Another time Milton came at me outside of The Ship Inn and that must have been about the sixth fight I'd had with Milton that year. Yet again Milton's moving about like Frank Bruno and suddenly, I seen this turnip waving at me, it must have been Halloween time, so I picked up the turnip, which was on a string and started battering him to death with the turnip and he went down unconscious. Colin Carney was stood watching it and he shouted, "YOU'RE ROUND THE FUCKING BEND DICKO". I went and smashed the windows of his BMW as he was asleep on the floor.

Me and Milton did make it up years later but if you're reading this Milton I still remember the score, its 17 – 2 to me.

One thing Milton did, which really pissed me off, was when he came to my house once with a baseball bat, but I had the sense not to open the door. The next day I dressed in disguise and let five shots off at his house and he never came to my fucking house anymore after that. I don't want to humiliate Milton as we're friends but the truths the truth. My friend Barry Suggett even said to Milton one day "If you walk down a certain street and a dog keeps biting you what do you do? You stop going down it so keep away from Terry Dicko!" People used to say to him for years "Watch out Dicko's about" like they used to do about Jeremy Beadle.

One night I was in the Ship Inn with Robert Suggett, Kevin Hawkes and the late Kevin Auer and we'd all been drinking. Anyway, I called to my house and I suppose I was showing off because I got my gun and fired a few shots and shouted, "THE MILKY BARS ARE ON ME". Everybody who was there was laughing. We then went out and got pissed some more but that was a stupid silly thing to do. I've never really been involved with guns. Any guns I ever had were disposed of.

Over the years I've been asked by people to get them guns, but I wouldn't dream of it. I was once remanded to Holme House prison for two months for allegedly shooting a house up which was completely shite. I lost two months of my life being incarcerated for something I had never done and that's still a sore one today. Of course, the charges were thrown out because I didn't do it but what's done is done and I can't get that time back.

In that time, I had some very good friends who sent me money in like Baldy Kelly and Ronnie Allan among others. I received the sum of £600 in two months which isn't too bad. I was helped by so many from inside of prison and its help in situations like that that will leave a lifetime of respect for someone.

When you're in prison having a sense of humour helps and most of the time I can't help but have a laugh.

As I've said having a sense of humour has always been a huge part of my life and it didn't matter what age I was, from being 10 to 60 I've always had a sense of humour.

One of the funniest things, off the top of my head, that I've ever done was the time I was stealing lemonade when I was about 10. I saw the guards bike parked up against the wall when I saw another fella passing by, and I shouted, "ERE MR DO YA WANT A FREE BIKE?" now that got his attention. He came over and said he did. Well I said, "That's my bike there but I don't want it anymore as it's my birthday tomorrow and my Mam is buying me a new one". Well the lad thanks me and off he rides away on this fabulous free bicycle happy as Larry, unfortunately the guard saw him and started chasing after him screaming "You twat you've stolen my bike". This bought me just enough time to run in and thieve a few bottles of lemonade and I ran off laughing and I went and sat in a field guzzling the lemonade with a smile on my chops. I'm surprised I didn't drown on pop that day.

Of course, there's always been many prostitutes plying their trade over the border and often as a lad, I'd be dropping stones on their heads, while they were doing their dirty deeds, like the cranes hand in a cuddly toy machine for a chase.

Kevin Pearson, my friend, had a dog named Rex and he brought it when he helped me paint my pigeon shed. Now years ago, Rex, the bastard, bit me and although I'm a big lover of animals I couldn't help but paint three sergeant stripes on the dog's shoulders when Kevin wasn't looking, and the dog mooched off home leaving just me and Kevin. Anyway, when Kevin left my house he returned around twenty minutes later ranting like

Yosemite Sam from the cartoon and I couldn't understand a word he was saying. I said, "Calm down what's the matter with you Kevin?" He said, "You know what the matter is you painted sergeant stripes on Rex". I said, "I wouldn't do such a thing like that I love animals". He said "Get out here now I'm gonna punch your face in" etc etc.... I said, "Well get your coat off then!" As soon as he tried to take his coat off I tangled him up in it and pinned him to the floor and punched his head in. He didn't offer me out again but that was just me being funny and having a laugh, I didn't mean any harm, but he took it the wrong way.

One funny story I have from my adult life was when the snooker player Alex Higgins came to the Steam Packet, now that was hilarious. To watch him and my late friend Franky 'Tenner' Mckenna rolling around the floor over a joint Alex was smoking. What happened was Franky said to Alex that he wanted a draw, Alex has then told him to fuck off and called him an English bastard in his distinguishable Irish accent. Franky said, "Don't be like that Alex I was a big fan of yours back in the day". Franky being the ever-persistent little cunt he was tried to grab the joint and Alex was just as quick, and he hung on to it, next thing you know they were both rolling around the floor. At one moment Alex's Crombie overcoat was flapping and it looked like he was mounting Franky. God, I wish camera phones were about in them days as if they had been it would have made the News of The World. It was the funniest thing I've ever seen. In the end little Kevin Auer broke it up and took Alex to the toilet and gave him a line.

Franky would always pester me for coke and although I wasn't really into coke I'd often say yes and what I'd do is go and crush a big pile of salt up and I'd say to him do you want a big line or a little line and because he was that greedy he'd ask for the big, so did his friends. I'd watch him have a good sniff and his eyes would be watering and the next minute my eyes would be watering too, and I'd be doubled up with laughter.

Another funny story I have of Franky was in the Packet when he was in a sexual clinch with a girl and things were about to go to the next level, that was until I blasted the pair of them with the foam hosepipe. Everybody was crying.

Once I was at a well known venue in Middlesbrough when I walked in and caught the full band, who were very popular at the time, powdering their noses. The lead singer made some arsey comment to me to close the door on the way out. Well as I couldn't go for him I picked up the fire extinguisher again and I was gonna blast him until my friend Robert talked me out of it. Things weren't going to get better for them that night if I wasn't talked out of it by my pal.

One night in The Havana with lip up fatty singer Buster Blood Vessel was funny but maybe not for me at the time. Now his song 'Lip up fatty' has a special meaning to me and I'll tell you why. Now Buster Blood Vessel had been playing a gig at the polytechnic and he comes in The Havana with his trademark Hawaiian shorts on and braces hanging down. So, me for a laugh sneaked up behind him and pulled his pants down. He turned around like lightning and punched me right in the lip, so I fucking grabbed him by his bald head and we were rolling around the floor. After our little fight we both stop, and he asks me my name which I tell him. He then says how sorry he was and that he was tired after his gig. He did tell me that if he started getting his pants pulled down once a week then everyone would start doing it and it would happen a hundred times, so please could I not do it again. I said sorry and we had a pint together.

Another time I was in London with John Miller and we saw Simon Le Bon with his beautiful wife Yasmin. Anyway, John decided to shout to Simon "May I give your wife a kiss?" Simon shouts back" CERTAINLY NOT". I shouted back "WELL YA BARRED OUT THE PACKET SIMON!" All the other Boro folk there died laughing but of course Simon Le Bon didn't have a clue what I was banging on about.

I was once told by someone that my best mate Nosha Howard was given a good hiding by a doorman for nothing so me, absolutely raging and wanting revenge, flew out the house and smashed the fucker's car up with a hammer. The next day I rang Nosha, all proud of myself and I told him "Don't worry mate I've done that fuckers car, so you just get better Nosh, ok". He paused a long pause and said, "Terry what are you on about?" I said, "That cunt who brayed you last night I've went and wrote his car off for you!" He said, "Nobody has battered me Terry I wasn't even out last night!" I'd like to apologise to whoever's car that was now, please forgive me.

I'm very well-travelled for your average fella from over the border i.e. Barbados, Gambia, Antigua, Dominican Republic, Florida, Turkey, Benidorm, Goa, Cuba, Mexico and all on my ill-gotten gains from one little fiddle or another.

In Gambia there was a load of crocodiles on the edge of the river and me being game didn't give a fuck and I stepped over them, these big fuckers with huge teeth, everything was a doddle until my daft mate Nosha Howard kicked the crocodile between my legs which severely pissed the croc off and I absolutely shit myself. Nosha was laughing his head off because he'd just nearly had me eaten alive by wild crocodiles.

Whilst we're on about crocodiles, I'll tell you about the time when I was in India and there was a ten foot croc on the bank. Now, I didn't believe it was a real one, I thought it was a big plastic model and I was about to jump in until at the last minute I seen it crawl down towards me. That still scares me today thinking about it. I was about to jump in and Terry Dixon would have been no more.

Going back to that twat Nosha and wild animals, we were both in Gambia and we saw this big strong Lion, there was only a wire fence about 8ft tall separating us from it. As Nosha walked past he kicked the fence shouting "HELLO LEO HELLO LEO" and it barged for the pair of us. Again, Nosha thought it was funny and he did the same shotting nuts at a wild monkey with the biggest teeth I ever saw. You need danger money just being that man's friend.

I once got fixed up in Rumours nightclub in the early 80s and we went behind the Wellington pub for obviously you know what for. As we've finished I noticed a tea towel on the line. So, I've grabbed the towel to wipe myself and when I'd finished I chucked the towel on the floor. The next night I wondered in a little kebab shop and as the man comes from the kitchen to come out and take my order I notice the towel from the night before across his shoulder. I said, "Hang on a minute mate I'll just go find out where my mates are" and I ran around the corner having a right laugh. Needless to say, I never went back and ordered anything. I do wonder if I went on to contaminate half of Middlesbrough that weekend.

I think by now you'll be able to tell I've been very passionate about my border roots, but I do miss all the great St Hilda's pubs. One day in the fleece public house Brian Hall kept chewing me, at the time I was playing pool with a friend of mine called Kestrel for a fiver, so the odds were big, and the pressure was on. "Brian stop fucking about being a nuisance" I told him, but he wouldn't, so I've turned around and pushed him over and his head hit the wall. He was out before he hit the floor. Now me being a mischievous cunt pulled his pants down and put a fag between his arse cheeks and lit it. When he woke up he went berserk and smashed the pub up so The Fleece barred me out and I said, "What am I barred out for?" "You caused that" was the answer the landlady replied with. I said he was chewing me, and I lashed out, but it fell on deaf ears. Anyway, I lost my patience and said FUCK YOU and walked out in disgust. The next day I tipped a barrow full of horse shit on The Fleece doorway just before it opened. They phoned the police, but they couldn't prove it was me. Anyway, the next day I walked in the pub again and ordered a drink, but they phoned the police again. I said "Yeah, I'll go but I'll be back tomorrow" before making my departure. Anita who had it, god bless her, has gone but her and Dicky McGlynn let me back in because they were that sick of me. In the end she said, "You're not going to go away are you?" I said, "No because I hadn't done anything in the first place". Anita said "YOU'RE A CHEAKY BASTARD DICKO" then asked me what I wanted to drink, and I was allowed back in.

The fella who I mentioned earlier who I was playing pool with was Kestrel and he's a great lad. His nicknames Uncle Fester Ford Fiesta. Kestrels fucking mad and he'd play on the one arm bandits in the Western social club and when he'd lose he'd fling it over. Many times, I'd walk past Kestrel playing on the fruit machine and he'd be having a dance with it, rocking it from side to side.

"Friends and good manners will carry you where money won't go". - Margaret Walker

17

Young Guns

As I've already said violence has always been in and around my life for many years. Even when at times I haven't had much choice about it. It hasn't only been the pub brawls either at times it's been far scarier than that, like an incident over the border about 2006.

I was in my car and I cut through a gap which lead to the back of my house. As I was parking my car up I noticed a gang of lads at the top of the street and at that time one of my neighbours was having a load of chew with a certain gang. As I went onto Stockton Street I noticed the same gang drove past me going up and down the street and their eyes were all over, I just had a sense that they were up to no good.

I've always been very observant of what is going on around me. I suppose with the things I've done in my life it's been built into me like second nature.

As I turned into West Street this car pulled around again, but I kept on walking to Suffield Street and the car still followed. Now I've become slightly paranoid and I turned around to see five lads in their twenties jump out of the car with guns in their hands and they were all shouting "DIXON YOUR GONNA GET IT!" Looking back, it was fucking foolish, in fact it was damn right crazy, but I ran towards them and shouted back "I'LL FUCKING GIVE YOU THIS" by which I meant a claw hammer that I had hold of because I'd been fixing my Sisters fence in a nearby house. Now I don't know what I expected a claw hammer to do in the first place against five guns but that's the truth. I don't want people to read this and think he's full of shit but that's the truth. I just didn't give a fuck for the consequences.

The five lads just laughed and started banging the bottom of their guns implying that they were loaded for me. I just laughed and shouted, "OH FUCK OFF" and turned around and walked in my sisters. When I got in my sister's home I told her what had gone on outside just now, so she went to have a look, but they'd fucked off sharpish.

Years later I was sat in the company of one of the five men and he said to me "We were warned not to fuck about with you Terry". He said, "You've got some fucking bottle you running at five men with guns". I told him to just forget it and we were all friends and I meant it. I think them five lads were shocked, and I out manoeuvred them in psychology.

All that was really over was a battle that people in that area were having with this gang, it was nothing to do with me it was all to do with drugs and drugs have never been my scene.

Over the years I've had my run ins with this family which meant my car 'mysteriously' caught fire and occasionally

I'd hear guns going off outside my house which I was meant to hear. I did my own share of damage to the people behind it in various little incidents that occurred. That feud saw me do two months on remand as I've mentioned in here on another page.

I did forgive that lad that night because he was only a young lad and as I always say, let he who is without sin cast the first stone like it says in the bible.

I've done more wrong than most people and sometimes I still haven't learnt my lesson at 61. God forgive me and forgive them. My ill feeling history with that family is over.

It was only weeks before that the boss at The Ship Inn, Peter, told me that there'd been somebody in his bar with a shot gun and balaclava looking for me shouting "TELL DICKO HE'S DEAD" but he told me he was sure it was Colin Leadbetter. Leadbetter was a right little shit and the first opportunity I got to see him was in the Bongo with Tommy Harrison. I walked up to Leadbetter and I said, "It was you with the shotgun wasn't it?" He wouldn't admit it at first, but I put on my friendliest act and told him it didn't matter anymore because we were all friends here. I told him I wasn't bothered about it, I knew it was him because Peter recognised his voice, which he hadn't. I just made that bit up to make him feel like the walls were closing in so that he'd admit it. Anyway, he said, "Yeah Terry it was me" and within a second of him telling me that I gave him such a fucking backhander which nearly took his head off and he ran out of the club. I chased after him out on to the street telling him what I thought of him. He was screaming that he just wanted to talk to me, but I told him to fuck off. He'd come looking for me with a loaded gun only a few weeks before, I didn't want to be his mate and I didn't want him anywhere near me! I told him he should be wary of what I would do to him if I saw him again and he was off. Truth be told I let it go and it's now been years since that happened.

I'm a firm believer that people who are going to shoot you don't go pulling guns out and letting the world know it's going to happen. A serious threat would be from the ones who say nothing and hide in a bush or behind a wall and do it. He was just a joke!

Another time in The Bongo I clashed with Grove Hill's Stevie Shannon and the next day he came to my house saying he had a shot gun in the boot of his car and if I let my Rottweiler's out he was gonna shoot them. Heated words were exchanged that day between me and him but in the end, we became friends. Steve Shannon is a lovely lad and that's how our friendship was made.

I have seen people being shot in life and being seriously damaged. I was there when Jamie Broderick was shot in the leg in The Bridge Inn. Davie Allo was there and sprayed some CS gas then poor Jamie took one in the leg by a well known Middlesbrough man who's name I won't mention.

Violence at all levels is very unattractive on the eye even though I was happy to use anything at hand against my enemy at that time, be it a wall brick, pint glass, ash tray, knife or a Halloween turnip. When you got involved in a fight on Teesside you had to do anything to stay alive.

When I was a boy my Mother used to tell me and my brothers if anybody hit us we must hit them back. Then if we weren't capable of beating them we should pick a stick up. Well that was very much ingrained into me and has stayed with me even to this day. As a boy it was sticks and stones and as I've gotten older and the games have become madder, so have the choice of weapons so now it would be more bricks and guns possibly even running people over!

As I've said many times over the years I never gave a fuck for the consequences and when I look at some lads in Middlesbrough doing big sentences, at times I feel very guilty because I should be where they are. I can only put it down to luck that I'm not doing a ten stretch myself. I can only thank god for the way my life has gone so far.

So many people over the years in our town have asked me to get into all sorts when they've been full of drink or drugs. I have always declined because I never got myself involved in talking shit. It's the same when people come to me and say, "See him there" etc etc, I'd always say "STOP STOP STOP, if you're not gonna tell them then please don't tell me because I'll go tell them".

One funny fucker who was gossiping about a couple of my friends I ended up knocking out with a range pan. I wouldn't mind I quite liked the lad, but he was just slagging all my friends off and wouldn't shut up.

"Good manners will open doors that the best education cannot". - Clarence Thomas

18

Charity begins at Home

The good people on Teesside know about Terry Dicko the dangerous bastard. Terry Dicko who at times has been into everything, but not many people will know the Terry Dicko who's done so much charity work and community work. As I told you all at the start of my book, I had marvellous parents. When I was a child my Dad wouldn't just buy me an ice cream he'd buy all the kids in the street one also. My son Terry Junior takes after him in his generous ways, he goes to the NSPCC and gives them £500 each year. All our family have had that good attitude of helping people.

One day I was at work and found an old bike which had just been left. Well I picked it up and done it up to give to a little Asian kid in my road. To see his face lit up when I gave him it was the only thing I wanted out of it. I got it for nothing, spent about four hours doing it up and passed it on and that was very rewarding for me.

Many years ago, when the kid next door to me got ran over I went out and asked all the lads over the border who are stealing cars and going joyriding to stop it. I asked them nicely but that didn't work so I asked them not so nicely and told them straight! "You better fucking

160

stop it or else". A few of them, after I told them were still taking the piss, so I got my nephew Daniel to get my brothers JCB from his skip business and I got him to put big lumps of sandstone at the bottom of the street to stop it and that put an end to it.

Another time one of the kids, Daniel Dowson, asked me if I wanted to buy some wood. Now this wood was ideal to make a picnic bench for St Hilda's, so I told him I'd have it. He told me he wanted £20 for it and I pulled £20 out and he went to grab it with the arms of an Octopus. I said, "It's not that easy!" He then got a bit annoyed and said, "Do you want the wood or not?" I told him that I did but that I wanted him to make the picnic bench out of it. Well he said to me he didn't have the first idea on how he would do that, but I told him he could, because I'd help him. So, I spent two and a half hours with Daniel showing him how to make a picnic bench. I had one in my garden I'd made earlier around my fish pond. I used to have a load of Koi Carp which brought back memories of 'Grandad' the fish who was stolen from me as a lad. To cut a long story short, when that kid finished making the picnic bench he was as proud as a Peacock.

The next day I saw him telling all of his friends that he made it and if anyone ever does anything to it he'd kill them. To me that was music to my ears because not only did he get £20 off me but Daniel created something that he was very proud of. Sometimes I would see old age pensioners coming over to sit on Daniels bench on Nile Street.

Another day I had all the kids in the area planting shrubs around the bench. A lovely friend of mine named Gail Fields, who I absolutely love, gave us some funding towards some things and I had all the kids painting the old Gladstone pub which was on the corner of Stockton Street to brighten the area up.

Me and the St Hilda's kids also made a badminton court from funding from my friends Andy Picko and Mick Dunn. Swing balls that were salvaged from my brother's skips were put up and put to good use. I also built them a log cabin, running track and BMX track. The biggest mistake I made was that I donated a dozen golf clubs and a few hundred golf balls to the kids. Them golf balls ended up bouncing off passing trains from the kids thinking that they were the next Tiger Woods. I got one of my friends, Stevie Bell, who is a tremendous artist to write on the wall 'We're angels with dirty faces not the dead-end kids' which is from the James Cagney film. Too many people in Middlesbrough saw us as the dead-end kids, which of course we weren't. Even the mayor of Middlesbrough and former top cop Ray Mallon came out to give us his approval.

I won an award and was invited to the Champion of The North Awards and ended up being a runner up. I also won the 'Taking a stand' award for my community work and for all the work I've done taking a stand against anti-social behaviour. I suppose it doesn't really tie in with my record now of smashing an egg off the MP of Middlesbrough, but shit happens.

Even today those kids who I helped back maybe 15 years ago and who are all grown up now haven't forgotten me. When I walk in the pub many of them have come rushing over asking to buy me a pint for the help I'd given them as kids. That really does make my heart warm and I do love that. I was even invited to the Houses of Parliament and I went.

I have a funny story about visiting the Houses of Parliament. I went with my friend Gail who I mentioned earlier. Now Gail borrowed a bag off her sister not realising that it had an 8 inch knife in a special compartment. The reason it was in Gail's sisters' bag in the first place was because her car broke down and she needed the knife to cut the rope it was towed away with. Anyway, she gave Gail the bag and when she went to walk into the House of Commons it flagged up straight away on the machine. So, this big huge guard came out and said, "Is this your bag" and Gail confirmed it was, well the guard said, "What's this" and pointed to the knife. Gail looked shocked and I just started laughing. Gail had never seen it in her life. Anyway, the guard said he'd keep hold of it until we came back out. He must have thought she wanted to go kill a few MP'S on her visit, you couldn't make it up but that's true. So, we went through to the awards and afterwards we had some lovely sandwiches with many of the famous toffs and we had a great day. On the way out, the security asked Gail if she wanted her knife back in front of everyone! Needless to say, Gail left her knife there and scurried out in a hurry. I often watch the debating chamber on the news and I say to Leslie "I've been there and sat in that spot". Not many people can say that, especially a scally like me from over the border.

I've also done a lot for Middlesbrough council. One story that comes to me when I say this was a lady called Marie whose child was disabled, and I did her garden up for her, so she had better access. Ste Spensley and Barry Faulkner gave me money to buy all chip barks, so it was soft for the bairn and to help this family. To be honest Marie turned out to be a nightmare for me, she turned out to be a monster, but I didn't do it for her and that's another story. I did it for her child, so I don't regret it although she wasn't worthy of the good cause, but it was god's work as I call it, and I suppose it will earn me a few brownie points for when my time comes in case I go down to the bad fire(laughs).

I really enjoy going out of my way and helping people, even as a lad maybe 18-19-year-old.

When I was just a lad I knew a nice old fella who used to go collect all the empty cardboard boxes from the fruit shop where the flyover was near where the Last Orders pub is. Now he also used to collect the thin slats from the wooden boxes which the shops kept the cabbages in, which were, of course, for his open fire to heat his full house. He lived near my Mam's house in West Street and he usually walked around with two coats on because he couldn't afford the heating. I would walk past and look in and I'd see him trying to get his fire going and my heart went out to him. So, one day I went out and got my pick-up van and filled it with logs from somewhere, they weren't pinched, but I never paid for them. Anyway, I chopped it all up and I knocked on his door, "Ere Pop, there you are". He said to me "I've got nowhere to put it all Terry" but I filled his bath up with it. I don't think he was getting a bath anyway god bless him. That was purely goodness from me, nothing more and that's how it should be. I tell you what, that gave me such pride and pleasure. His house was lit up like Santa's grotto for a month.

I'm always looking to get involved in projects so if you're reading this and you need a hand then come and see me, I mean that sincerely. I'm not the monster that certain folk in Middlesbrough make out that I am!

"Never look down on anybody unless you're helping them up" - Imam Ali

THANKS

I have had many friends who have been there for me over the years such as my best mate Nosha Howard. Nosha was there for me when I was stuck as was Carl McCarton, Kenny 'The Phone', Docko, Bram (Chris Crossan) who I always knew had a good heart before he found Jesus, Big Anth from The Zetland Door, John Graham, Buster Atkinson, big Peter McGee, Tony Robbo who has been good to me, Rod from The Ship Inn, Rob Train, Kenny Howard, My friend Martin Henry(H) who died the night I'd just left him. I loved H and it gave me some comfort that we'd had a good laugh the night he died, God bless you my big friend. Jimmy Mac from Seaham who's one tough fucker and I finally forgive him for pinching my pen in jail. He says I tried to get in bed with him still to this day.

I'd like thank Jamie Boyle for doing my friend Lee Duffy's book and doing him justice. The first time I met Jamie he was 19 and told me to 'Fuck Off' a dozen times in the Steam Packet, his naivety saved him that night (laughs). Danny Blackley who's one mad fucker with a cock the size of a wasp's, Robert Suggett, Lee and Ste Spensley who've been there for me, Mark Paylor also deserves a mention. Lee Duffy's close friends, Neil Booth, Mark Hartley along with Mark's son Liam, I still regard these men as good friends even though, since Lee's passing, we don't see each other often, our unequivocal love and respect for Lee will always bond us.

Only last week my little pal "Bonk" came to my aid as some clown was trying to look for bother with me, even though Bonk is getting on for 65, the old cunt, he still expressed his concerns for me. The guy should consider himself lucky as "Bonk" was a good boxer in his youth, he should also consider himself lucky that I didn't turn on him myself.

Thanks also, to my nephew Craig Nettleton who has really been a support to me at times and I love him dearly. My children, I love them all and my son Terry Junior who makes me proud every day. I feel very honoured to have made a new found friend in Paul Duffey, who I came to know while writing this book. I have to give you this mention Paul and you've turned out to be a great guy.

I have to mention my love for my Cousin Neil Fairclough and John 'Winky' Watson, who are both proper lads and I perhaps don't see them as often as I should. Love to you both.

I hope you've all enjoyed 'Laughter, Madness and Mayhem'. Anybody who purchased this book I thank you from the bottom of my heart I really do, now come and have a fucking pint with me.

This book is my way of shedding my demons because I can't apologise for the rest of my life and I just hope now people believe me and I can move on. I am the little bastard from over the border after all.

Coming in 2019 from Warcry Press

Lee Duffy
'The Blood Moon'

ISBN:TBC

by Jamie Boyle

Follow up to the Amazon Best Seller

'Lee Duffy – The Whole of The Moon'

*From the author of the best selling Paul Sykes books
'Unfinished Agony' and 'Further Agony' Jamie Boyle.*

Also available from Warcry Press

Lee Duffy
'The Whole of The Moon'

ISBN: 978-1-912543-07-6

by Jamie Boyle

A book which has taken over 25 years to arrive. The definitive story of the man who held an eight year reign of terror over the town of Middlesbrough.

Containing many first hand and previously unheard accounts from some of Duffy's closest friends and associates, this book will finally confirm who the man was and what he was really all about.

No stone will be left unturned and this book will not shy away from controversy, but will aim to provide an unbiased and balanced view on the 'Borough icon .

Make no mistake, this will be the definitive book on Lee Duffy, there will be no more 'ifs' and 'buts after its release.

From the author of the best selling Paul Sykes books 'Unfinished Agony' and 'Further Agony' Jamie Boyle.

Also available by Jamie Boyle

Sykes: Unfinished Agony

ISBN: 978-0-9955312-4-6

Paul Sykes, from Lupset, near Wakefield, died aged 60 in Pinderfields Hospital from pneumonia and cirrhosis of the liver. He was a man whose life might have been changed by success in the boxing ring, but despite contending for the British & Commonwealth Heavyweight Titles, he sank back into old habits. It heralded a return to the self-destructive course of his life. By 1990, he had spent 21 out of 26 years in 18 prisons and even as recently as 2006 he was still coming to the attention of the law. His years in prison were not entirely wasted. He earned an Open University degree in Physical Sciences, and his book Sweet Agony, which was re-released in 2015, earned the Arthur Koestler prize for prison literature.

This book is my journey to find out what happened to Paul Sykes between the years after his 1990 cult classic documentary Paul Sykes at Large aired on the First Tuesday programme and his eventual tragic demise in 2007. I've interviewed many people that knew Paul both personally and professionally and I have tried to achieve a balanced view of who he was and what he was about.

As someone who set out, just out of interest, to find out what happened to this character after the limelight had left him behind I'm satisfied that as well as many stories from his younger days I've managed to piece his last 17 years together. This book has caused a bit of controversy as it doesn't shy away from the truth and it hasn't always been easy to hear people's points of view about Paul but I hope it gets across his huge personality both the good and bad. It's been a Roller-Coaster to say the least.

Also available from Warcry Press

Tales of Pugilism

ISBN: 978-1-912543-03-8

by Jamie Boyle

A unique look into the lives of some of the key players in and around the boxing world.

Featuring many well known faces, asking how they first got involved in boxing? and what it means to them.

With many inside stories it reveals a side to boxing one often doesn't see.

Written by Jamie Boyle author of Paul Sykes books, Unfinished Agony and Further Agony, it will be a hard hitting boxing book for sure.

Includes:

Kevin Mitchell, Davey Robinson (Repton ABC), Matthew Burke, Andrew Buchanan, Richie Horsley, Alex Morrison, Colin Hart, Joe Maphosa, John Spensley, Francis Jones, Matt Hamilton, Alan Temple, Dominic Negus, Peter Richardson, Josh Warrington, Jon Lewis Dickinson, Bradley Welsh, Nick Manners, Gary Sykes, John Pearce.

Also available by Jamie Boyle

Further Agony:
'One More Round with Sykes'

ISBN: 978-0-9955312-6-0

by Jamie Boyle

The sequel to the Amazon best seller 'Unfinished Agony' The 3rd and final book on the wild man of Wakefield Paul Sykes.

Further Agony includes chapters from: Delroy Showers; Davy Dunford; Josie Threlfall; Chris Lambrianou; Harry Lakes; Reg Long; Dave Owens; Neil Atkinson; Janet Sellers; John Purvis; Tom Kiely; Colin Hart; Lance Jackson; Alan Lord; Clyde Broughton; Mark Sellers; Alan Brown; Mark Szedzielarz; Kenny Williams; Tommy Harrison; David Flint; Wes Bostock; Simon Ambler; Ricky Wright-Colquhoun; Tracy Thompson; Andy Hammond; Shaun First; Janet; Danny Leach; Julie Abott; Gary Mills; Imran Hussain; Lee Daniels; Dean Ormston; Wakefield Police Officer.